WHEN GOD CHEERS

WHEN GOD CHEERS

The story of a father, a daughter and the stranger who changed their lives during a magical season

JOHN SHAUGHNESSY

Corby Books
Notre Dame, Indiana

WHEN GOD CHEERS
Copyright © 2014 John Shaughnessy

All rights reserved. No part of this book may be used or reproduced in any manner whatsoever without the written permission of the publisher.

10 9 8 7 6 5 4 3 2 1

ISBN 978-0-9890731-8-9

Manufactured in the United States of America

Published by Corby Books
A Division of Corby Publishing
P.O. Box 93
Notre Dame, Indiana 46556
(574) 784-3482
www.corbypublishing.com

To John, Brian and Kathleen

Acknowledgments

At its heart, this story is about the relationship between a parent and a child. The inspirations for this story are my three children—who are also my favorite athletes of all time. Even more, they are great gifts in my life because of the people they are. Thank you, John, Brian and Kathleen, for the tremendous blessing of being your father. In that same spirit, I give thanks to my mom and dad, Doris and John Shaughnessy, who have always been their children's biggest fans.

At its heart, this story is also about friendship. With this book, I've been fortunate to have the help of many longtime friends and a few new ones. Special thanks to John Byers, Steve Dickmeyer, Juanita Dix, Jon Grant, Darrin Gray, Jim Langford, Clark Power, Kathy Malone Sparks, Emily and Larry Connolly, Dan and Joyce Wagner, and my best friend, my wife Mary. Your support, guidance and encouragement make a great difference.

At its heart, this story is also about the people who become part of our lives through our children's involvement in sports. I'm grateful to the coaches who have helped shape the lives of my children. My admiration and appreciation also extend to their teammates who have shared the fun, the hard work, the dreams and the memories with them. Thank you also to all the parents I have cheered alongside through the years. The dreams and efforts of our children—and our dreams and efforts for them—unite us.

A Confession

Many of his friends call him "God."

Considering what he has done for me, I think of him as a friend, too—maybe the best one I've ever had—but I've never felt comfortable calling him by that nickname.

Like many nicknames that guys give each other, his came through a combination of a defining trait, a touch of good-natured humor and—this point can't be stressed enough—a true appreciation for him as a person. After his nickname was explained to me, I understood why they had given it to him. And I also understand why other people consider it irreverent and even blasphemous to use that nickname for a person.

But here's my confession. At a time when I desperately needed someone to help me see what truly mattered in life, he was there for me. And he helped me in such a rare, giving, funny and creative way that I have to admit that I sometimes wondered if he was sent by God or if. . .

It's just that his unusual, sudden appearance in my life dovetailed with the two areas—sports and faith—where I've always been taught to believe in this one extraordinarily common reality: *Anything is possible.*

A child born in a stable. Water turned into wine. A Hail Mary touchdown pass. The Immaculate Reception. The blind man getting his sight back. The Cinderella Man getting his fight back. The miracle of the loaves and fishes. The miracle of the 1980 United States' hockey team. And above all, a man who rose from the dead.

So I know in my heart and I believe in my soul that anything is possible. Yet, I'm still trying to make sense of everything that happened during that special season. Right now, I'm just certain of one point: I was on the verge of losing one of the most important people in my life when I first met him.

"God" as a Sports Fan

Before I tell you about the first time I met him—a time that ended with me telling him, "Get the hell away from me"—there are a few things you might be interested in knowing about him as a sports fan.

He always eats popcorn when he watches a game in the stands.

He usually sits in the middle of a crowd, enjoying being in the midst of other fans, and often watching them with as much interest as the players.

Even when the score is lopsided, he never leaves a game until it's finished, because he believes that wondrous moments can happen even when time and hope are fading away. "Besides," he says, "I always like to watch how people react to winning and losing. You learn a lot about them that way."

He enjoys—and often flashes a huge smile—when athletes make a special play. But he also sighs or turns silent when players follow it by pounding on their chests, striking a pose or doing

3

anything else that basically proclaims, "Look at me!" At the same time, he quietly nods in appreciation when players subtly point to the heavens, especially if it seems to be a salute to a loved one who has died, or as recognition that their talent has been given as a gift by a higher power. He is "old school" that way, with one exception. When a player once celebrated by doing a standing back flip, I was stunned to see him smile and exclaim, "Wow!" So I asked him about his reaction. "You have to love the amazing things that people can do with their bodies," he said, flashing that smile.

He also loves to laugh. He especially appreciates when people laugh at themselves. He once told me an anecdote that legendary college football coach Lou Holtz often shared from his days as the coach of the University of Arkansas: "After one big victory when I was at Arkansas, I was put in the Arkansas Hall of Fame, and a stamp was issued with my name on it. But the next year, we lost to Texas, and they had to take me off the stamp. People were spitting on the wrong side."

He also enjoyed the reaction of a pro quarterback who suffered a dizzy spell during a game and had to undergo several medical tests—tests that led to a startling discovery for the player. After getting the results, the quarterback said, "They checked my head and found out I had a brain. That was real encouraging."

Then there is his most distinctive trait—the moments when he cheers. It took most of a season of watching games with him and listening to his stories—*he loves to tell and share stories*—before I realized that he only cheers at certain moments. Even more than great physical displays, he relishes those moments in sports when athletes give their heart and soul—showing how deeply they care about the game, their teammates, their coaches and, yes, even their opponents. Two of his favorite stories illustrate that last point. One involves an Olympic gold medalist. The other story focuses on a small boy playing his first game.

"Have you ever heard of Holly Metcalf?" he asked me once.

When I said, "No," he smiled. Then he began the story that Metcalf told when she was asked to share her most defining moment in sports.

"Holly could have just chosen the story of how she won an Olympic gold medal. She could have just talked about the race and the glory—the images of her teammates hugging her, and her friends and her family congratulating her. Instead, she recalled a moment when she stood alone, a moment that challenged her as a competitor and a person.

"On that day, Holly was six months removed from her gold-medal experience as a member of the United States' 8-women rowing team. Now, she was coaching that team in the world championships, desperately wanting to beat the favored Romanians. The Romanians had arrived at the world championships without a boat. All of their boats had been destroyed during a rebellion that left thousands of people dead and the eastern European country in turmoil. Holly could see the toll of that country's hardship reflected in the faces of the Romanian rowers. She also saw the choice she faced. Her U.S. team had an extra boat. If she didn't offer it to the Romanians, the Americans would dramatically increase their chances of winning the world title.

"So what did Holly do? She offered the boat. Naturally, the Romanians accepted. And the race that followed was everything a world championship should be.

"The Romanians and the Americans surged to the front, pushing each other with each stroke—an intense duel that had every rower in both boats straining for something more, something deeper, *something* yet-untapped inside them. It was the way Holly had raced in the Olympics. And every ounce of her strained again as she watched the battle on the water.

"In the end, the Romanian boat knifed across the finish line first, barely beating the Americans.

"Later, some people approached Holly and said, 'You would have won the gold medal if you hadn't given them the boat.' Holly just met their eyes and replied, 'That wasn't the point. I know it brought out the best in my team. The demands of a sport bring out your character and inner strength. Character in sports is everything.'"

When he finished that story, he didn't say anything else for a while. He just let Holly's point speak for itself. But there was no hiding the respect and the joy that glowed in his eyes. He had the same look when he later shared the story of a small boy playing his first baseball game.

"His name was Jimmy, and he was five years old at the time. As he walked toward home plate, he was naturally nervous. It was his first time ever at bat in a real game. Pausing for a moment, he looked out on a field where all the children shared a love for playing. They also shared some kind of physical disability.

"As Jimmy stepped into the batter's box, a man announced his name on the public address system, drawing applause from all the fans on the sidelines. No one cheered louder than Jimmy's mom and dad. Like all parents, they had been rooting for their only child every day of his life, and maybe even more so since he was diagnosed, 15 months after his birth, as having cerebral palsy.

"Back then, there was concern that Jimmy might never walk. And yet here he was, standing on his own two feet, playing baseball. So his parents' smiles and cheers didn't disappear when Jimmy swung and missed at the first couple of pitches. Then it happened. The ball came toward the plate fat and sweet, and Jimmy sent it sailing. He stood there beaming until everyone on the sidelines told him to run to first base. So he did. Then someone pointed him to second base as the fielders tried to pick up the ball. Reaching second, Jimmy kept running on legs reinforced by braces. Yet as he neared third base, he became winded.

"As the crowd shouted, 'Go, Jimmy! Go, Jimmy!' his mom could see he wanted to make it home. She could also see he was struggling. For a moment, she considered running to him, fearing he might fall. Before she could move, something wondrous happened. The other team's shortstop played his position from his motorized wheelchair. As his teammates finally picked up the ball and threw it toward home, the shortstop motored toward Jimmy. When he reached Jimmy, the shortstop said, 'Hop on back, I'll take you home.' Jimmy did, crossing home plate before the throw arrived.

"Getting off the wheelchair, Jimmy smiled and raised his arms above his head as the crowd and his parents cheered."

I've since shared that story with other people. It has made more than a few of them cry. That story has also made more than a few people wonder how I ever reached the point where I told this guy with the nickname of "God" to get the hell away from me. It happened at one of my daughter's basketball games.

How I Met "God," and Why I Told Him to Get the Hell Away from Me

Six seconds were left in the basketball game. Six seconds that would decide the outcome between the two arch-rival schools. My daughter had just driven down the lane in the tied game, a step ahead of her defender. As another girl on the other team tried to cut off my daughter's path, my daughter threaded a pass to an open teammate under the basket for the go-ahead score. When the opponent's head coach called timeout, my daughter's teammates and coaches rushed to her, congratulating her on the smart, unselfish play. Friends sitting next to me slapped me on the back and gave me high-fives while others farther away shouted their compliments about my daughter. I felt the pride surging through me again, the great feeling that always fills parents when their child does something special. It's a feeling that's especially strong for parents whose children play sports. At least it has always been that way for me.

Still, six seconds remained, plenty of time for the other team to have a shot at tying the game with a two-pointer or winning with a three. When the timeout ended, the other team inbounded the ball to their star player who rushed up the court with my daughter staying one step in front of her. With three seconds left, their star player crossed midcourt. At the three-point line, she stopped quickly, faked and launched a shot. Nearly everyone in the gym instinctively rose to their feet, watching the flight of the ball, but I kept my focus on my daughter and the shooter. When the girl had made her fake, my daughter had left her feet and bumped into the shooter. I heard the official's whistle before I turned to see the ball bounce off the rim as the buzzer sounded. The missed shot didn't matter. The official looked to the scorer's table, signaled a foul against number 15 on the blue team—my daughter—and raised his hand for three foul shots.

"What were you thinking?!" I said to myself about my daughter as the star player on the other team walked to the foul line. "How many times have I told you to never leave your feet on a shot fake?!"

The girl made the first shot to draw her team within one point. She tied the score a moment later with her second shot. I put my head down and closed my eyes for her third shot, praying that she missed. But the roar of the crowd from the other side of the gym let me know she had made it.

I sat down, my head in my hands, stunned, angry and nauseous. The friends and fans who had high-fived me and praised my daughter when there were six seconds left in the game now trudged past me. Most passed silently, but one said, "That's a shame," while another said, "There's no way a ref should make that call in that situation." I kept my head down, waiting for everyone to leave, but then I heard another set of footsteps crossing the wooden bleachers, heading in my direction.

He stopped right in front of me. I could see his white, high-top Converse Chuck Taylor sneakers and the bottoms of his khaki pants as he said, "I just want to tell you, that was a joy and a gift to watch your daughter play today. What a heart she has! She just gave *everything*! I'm sorry it didn't work out for her team today, but it must be so much fun for you to watch her play."

I should have thanked him for his words. I should have told him he was right about my daughter. Instead, I figured he was a parent from the other team, the kind of person who sometimes comes up to talk to you after a game that his child's team has just won. And he thinks he's being gracious and a good sport as he tells you what a great game it was and how great your child is, when all he's really doing is basking in the victory because he just wants that feeling to last as long as possible. In those moments, I've always had the urge to say, "Go away. I don't want to hear your joy. And I don't want to talk to you. Just leave. Right now." But I've never said those things until just then.

Without looking up at the stranger, I said, "Get the hell away from me."

At first, the white sneakers didn't move. But they soon turned, and I could hear him walking down the wooden bleachers toward the court. Finally, I lifted my head and looked around the gym. There was no one else left except the stranger and the gym manager, Dan, who was standing by one of the doors. The stranger walked toward the door, looked at Dan, and both their faces lit up with surprise and joy. They talked for about five minutes, smiling and laughing at times, before the stranger patted Dan on the shoulder and waved goodbye.

As I walked toward the gym door, Dan was still there. He knew me well enough to know I didn't want to talk about the game, but I never expected what he did say.

"I saw that 'God' stopped by to talk to you after the game," Dan said.

"What?"

"I said, 'I saw that 'God' stopped by to talk to you after the game.'"

"God?"

"Yeah, that's the nickname we gave him when he was a ref in basketball."

"Why?"

"He was the best ref I've ever worked with or seen," Dan said. "He just saw everything so clearly, he was always in the right position, and he never let his ego get in the way of calling a game. He also had a special way with the players and the coaches, even when they questioned him. He'd take the time to compliment them, explain something or calm them. And it got to the point where they just trusted that he was fair and wanted what was best for everyone on the court. And how about his voice? It's just this amazing blend of quiet command and joy. I've never seen or heard anyone like him."

"No one is that good, Dan," I said.

"*He* was," Dan said. "There was a ref on our crew named Jack Williams. Jack once said about him, 'He sees *everything*, he's always in complete control, and people have this great faith in him. And *that voice*. I tell you, if God was a ref, he'd be him.' Jack laughed as he said it, but the nickname stuck, and it caught on with some of the other refs. The strange thing was, he was just a ref for a few years, and then he walked away from it. It's been ten years, and this is the first time I've seen him since we last worked together."

"Is he related to someone on the other team?" I asked.

"No," Dan said. "He just said he picked this game out of the blue to come see. By the way, he just raved about your daughter."

"Yeah, he told me that, too. And I told him to get the hell away from me."

"What?!"

I tried to explain the situation to Dan, about how I thought his friend was a gloating parent from the other team, but it didn't matter. Dan looked stunned, and then he started laughing. "You told 'God' to get the hell away from you?!"

Dan kept laughing. That's when I saw my daughter waiting for me in the hallway outside the gym. I could see her shoulders sagging, and her eyes rimmed in redness and tears. I said goodbye to Dan and walked toward her. I should have comforted her. I should have told her how proud I was of her. I should have told her what the stranger had said about her. Instead, we walked to the car in silence. And on the way home, I did something far worse than tell a guy nicknamed "God" to get the hell away from me. I told my daughter, "You cost your team the game."

She cried as she ran into the house.

A Reason to Believe

"No! No! What are you doing?!" I shouted during the opening minutes of the next game.

My daughter had taken wild, off-balance shots the first three times her team had the ball, and each shot barely touched the rim before it was rebounded by a player on the other team.

"She needs to play under control," I said aloud to myself.

"She needs you to believe in her," said a voice from just behind me.

I turned and saw the man that my friend Dan had called "God." He didn't look at me though; his eyes were focused on the court.

"She tries so hard," he said. "That's one of the things I love about watching your daughter play."

"Trying is fine, but you have to make plays, you have to make shots. That's what matters," I barked, frustrated by her play and aggravated that he was here again.

"I know a lot of people agree with you," he said calmly.

On the court, my daughter dove for a loose ball and scooped it toward one of her teammates.

"But I love her effort," the voice behind me said as he stood and cheered for her.

Then the ball was passed back to my daughter. She quickly launched another wild shot that didn't even touch the rim. Her coach had seen enough. He turned to a player on the bench who soon went into the game as a substitute for my daughter. When my daughter came to the bench, her coach patted her on the shoulder.

"She's pressing," the man behind me said.

"She's playing awful," I responded. "I told her before the game that she had to take charge; that she had to take more shots if her team was going to win. And then she plays like this."

"She needs you to believe in her," he said again.

Hearing those words a second time was more than I could take.

"Listen, mister, I don't want to hear anymore from you," I said, feeling the anger surging through my body. "You don't know anything about my daughter and me. So just shut. . ."

"She believed in you when you needed it," he said.

"What?!"

"She believed in you when you needed it," he repeated.

"What are you talking about?"

"Think about it," he said. "It will come to you. Right now, popcorn sounds good to me. Want anything from the concession stand?"

I didn't answer him. Instead, I kept thinking about what he said, "She believed in you when you needed it." What was he talking about? I tried to put the thought aside and concentrate on the game, but I couldn't. Then I remembered the moment. It was a moment that had once connected my daughter and me in a way that I thought would never end.

It happened on a cloudless summer evening. My daughter was 10 then, a girl whose sun-streaked brown ponytail dangled from the back of a midnight-blue Detroit Tigers baseball cap. Actually, she had no allegiance to the major-league Tigers. The cap was just part of the uniform she wore when she played softball in a recreational league near our home. During that season, she often dragged me into our backyard to practice her pitching or to get some extra batting practice, taking great glee in thumping my pitches against the back of our white, two-story house. This was especially true when the extra-soft, practice softball rattled the kitchen window, which then led her suddenly-rattled mother to open the back door to chastise her suddenly-sheepish father about the wisdom of practicing in the backyard.

Such are the moments that bind a father and a daughter. And our bond became even tighter on that cloudless summer evening when she bounced into the living room wearing her baseball glove. My daughter, my wife and I were headed to watch the local minor league baseball team play at a stadium that often sells out its 13,000 seats. When my daughter was there a few weeks earlier with the family of a friend, a foul ball dropped from the sky, landed near her and bounced away, leading her to the firm belief that she shared with us in the living room. This time, with a glove on her hand, she was coming home with a souvenir baseball from the game.

Her faith has been shared by millions of baseball fans from different generations. Yet instead of sharing her belief, I, a lifetime fan, tried to lower her expectations. I told her that in all my years of attending professional baseball games, I had never come home with a souvenir game ball.

"Don't get your hopes too high," I said.

At 10, she looked at me like I was someone who had lost his sense of faith, his belief in the wonderful possibilities of life. And she was right. That summer, for reasons not related to her, I felt pain and loss where I once believed in hope and magic. Maybe she even sensed that change in me. Yet instead of giving into my doubt, she trumped it with a smile. So I headed to the closet where I keep my baseball glove and pulled it down from a shelf. Even if my belief in hope and magic had been shaken, there was no reason to rob my daughter of those gifts.

After spending four, no-foul-balls-in-our-direction innings in seats far down the left-field line, my daughter asked if we could relocate to the grassy sections that rim the outfield walls of the park. There, in a scene dripping with Americana, families and couples spread blankets, bring coolers and watch the game from gently sloping hills that overlook the field. We found an unclaimed spot of grass beyond the left field fence, father and daughter still wearing their baseball gloves yet only one of us believing. Then, in the midst of a scoreless pitchers' duel, came a series of events that would change one of our views.

When our team took the field late in the game, my wife suggested we should cheer and wave to the leftfielder as he headed to his position. So we did, getting a return wave from Izzy Alcantara, a Dominican-born baseball player who was in his fifth year of following his American dream of becoming a major league baseball player. When the home team came to bat later that inning, Izzy strolled to the plate. By then, I was routinely checking the electronic scoreboard in right-center field, noting the hitting statistics of each of the players at bat. Izzy's stats sent a wave of possibility and, inexplicably, hope through my mind. As I watched one of the team's leading home run hitters settle into the batter's box, I found myself rising from my sitting position and telling my daughter, "Get ready."

Seconds later, the ball rocketed off Izzy's bat in a high arc toward left field, drifting closer and closer to the fence. My daughter and I were both on our feet by then, drawn to the ball, focused solely on its flight against the backdrop of the stadium's glowing lights, unaware of anything or anyone else around us. It was a moment when part of your mind tells you this can't be happening, and another part wants to believe so much that it is.

Later that night, one of the local television stations would replay the scene that happened next at the game. The camera would show Izzy's shot carrying over the left field wall. It would also capture a man in a baseball cap and wearing a baseball glove moving toward the ball, with a young girl in a baseball cap and wearing a baseball glove at his side.

What the television camera didn't show was how graceful the man felt in that moment, how his heart raced in anticipation and expectation, how he felt like a 10-year-old child again, believing anything is possible. The camera also didn't capture the interaction between my daughter and me after Izzy's game-winning home run landed in my glove.

As the stadium erupted in cheers and fireworks, Izzy trotted toward home plate while I immediately handed the ball to my daughter.

"Thank you," she said.

I put my arm around her shoulder.

"Thank you," I told her.

That night, my daughter helped me believe in hope and possibilities again. That night, I started to believe in myself again.

With that night fresh again in my mind, I looked across the court to where my daughter sat at the end of the bench, looking miserable, looking like she had failed everyone who believed in her and depended on her.

I also scanned the crowd looking for the guy whose friends call him "God." I didn't see him. I wondered how he knew about the baseball game.

Courting Disaster

When it didn't seem like my relationship with my daughter could have become much worse, the following day it did.

In the afternoon, I saw her in the backyard of our house, taking shot after shot on the basketball goal in our driveway. It was a routine she followed every day. She usually took about 100 extra shots there, but the number normally increased after games during which she didn't shoot well. During those backyard practice sessions, I usually joined her. I rebounded the ball for her so she could spend more time shooting, and less time chasing after the ball. Through the years, those sessions had been a time we shared, a time that connected us.

As I watched her from a window where she couldn't see me, she hit most of the shots. Drawn to the scene and wanting to spend some time with her—and repair some of the damage I had done to our relationship—I walked outside and onto the court. I immediately fell into the rhythm of watching her shoot, getting the ball and passing it back to her. The more I did, the worse her shooting became. As I often had done during these sessions, I started making suggestions. "Your shot is flat. Add some arch to it." And, "Get your shoulders squared toward the basket when you shoot." After another miss and another suggestion, I passed the ball back to her. This time, she held the ball as she talked to me for the first time that day.

"I don't need you to be out here with me," she said. "I can do this by myself."

I started to say something, but I didn't. I just looked at her. In her eyes and her expression, I could see a blend of anger and hurt. I walked off the court and into the house, wondering why she couldn't understand that I just wanted to help her.

The First Letter from "God"

When I picked up my daughter after her basketball practice the next day, she barely spoke to me during our ride home. All my efforts to get her to talk—"How was practice today?", "Did your shooting improve?"—were answered with a mumbled "okay" or "I don't want to talk about it." At home, she headed straight for her room, saying she had "a ton of homework to do." I didn't see her again until right before dinner when she handed me an envelope.

"What's this?" I asked.

"I don't know," she said. "After practice, I was walking by Coach's office. Coach saw me and waved me in. He was talking to this man. Coach introduced me, and the man said he had met you at one of our games. He asked me to give you this."

She said everything tersely. When I looked at her, her eyes showed no warmth toward me. I wanted to say something to make it better between us, but she turned to leave. So I just quickly asked, "What did he look like?"

She sighed and stared at me. Still, she described him: "He's kind of tall, silver hair, and he wears these white, high-top sneakers. And he's got this distinctive voice. Just full of life. And he really focuses on you when he talks to you. He was nice."

By the time she finished describing him, her face and her voice had softened—at least in that moment.

"Did he or Coach Miller say how they knew each other?" I asked.

"No, but they were laughing about something when Coach saw me. It looked like they were friends. That's all I know. If that's all, I need to help Mom."

"Thanks," I said.

While my daughter went into the kitchen to help her mom, I walked to the living room with the envelope. Sitting back in a chair, I tore the envelope and opened the folded, hand-written note. As I began to read it, I noticed how clear and strong his penmanship was.

"I've been thinking about what you said at the last game, 'Trying is fine, but you have to make plays, you have to make shots. That's what matters.' One of my favorite quotes offers another perspective. It's from Mother Teresa. She said, 'God doesn't require us to succeed. He only requires that you try.'

"Another quote I've always liked is from Ralph Waldo Emerson, the American poet and philosopher. He said, 'To know even one life has breathed easier because you have lived. This is to have succeeded.'

"Emerson's quote reminds me of a story. It's the story of a guy named Gene Schmidt, and it begins when he was a teenager. His mother died of breast cancer when he was 14. His father lived in another part of the country. So Gene bounced around the homes of his older brother and sisters. No one in his family had graduated from high school. The rough part of town where he grew up overflowed with the kind of role models who enjoyed teaching a young guy how to steal a car and do other things that get the attention of the police. And when he went to high school, Gene didn't have a lunch or enough money to buy one in the cafeteria. So he took a special class called 'Food Preparation,' where he got to eat what he made.

"Tough. Poor. Humiliating. Dead-end. Choose any adjective you want to describe Gene's life at 17, or his future. There's no way he should have made it in life—and he believes he wouldn't have if it weren't for Herman Keller.

"Gene was a high school junior when he met Keller. Keller was a gym teacher and the school's junior varsity basketball coach. When Keller saw Gene play basketball in his gym class, he wanted him on the JV team. But there was one major obstacle to overcome. The varsity coach didn't want Gene on the JV team. He reasoned that Gene would just be taking playing time from younger players who eventually could help the varsity more. But Keller knew Gene's background. And he kept pushing for him, saying this could make a difference for the team *and* the kid. Finally, the varsity coach relented.

"By the next season, the varsity coach had left. Keller became the head coach. Gene became a starter on the team in his senior year, a season when their team won the state championship. That success was just the beginning for Gene. He earned a basketball scholarship to college, became a star there and met a young woman who later became his wife. He also earned a business degree that helped prepare him to start his own company.

"Years later, when he was looking back on his marriage, his career and his life, Gene said, 'It all goes back to a coach getting a runny-nosed kid on a team. None of this would have happened if he hadn't given me a start. My life has revolved around his teachings, his decisiveness, his love and compassion for me.'

"It's like Emerson said, 'To know even one life has breathed easier because you have lived. This is to have succeeded.'

"Take care."

It was the first of many notes I received from him that season. The next one he sent offered a glimpse of his sense of humor, including his ability to laugh at himself. It also included an invitation.

An Invitation

His second note came in the mail two days later, right between a bill from the electric company and a catalog from L.L. Bean.

"For a long time," he began, "I've collected all kinds of quotes from people. I like to know what other people think, and I like to share their thoughts and stories with my friends. Sometimes, my friends give me a hard time about using a quote from one part of life during a conversation about another completely different part of life. Maybe you had the same reaction when I used quotes from a Catholic nun and a 19th century American philosopher to talk about success in basketball. But I believe all parts of life are connected in one way or another. Still, that's a discussion for another time.

"In collecting quotes, I especially enjoy ones from people in sports because there's often a combination of humor and truth in their comments. Like there was the time a college football player was asked, 'If you could trade places with someone for a day, who would it be?' The player responded, 'Any female; then maybe I could figure them out.' And I love the response that another college football player gave when he was asked, 'If you had to be stranded on an island with just one person, who would you choose?' And the player answered, 'Someone who could build a boat.'

"Both their answers made me smile, and they also made me think. In both cases, the athletes recognized they needed some expert advice to reach where they wanted to be. In the same vein, All-Pro quarterback Peyton Manning said that his approach to sports comes from the example of his father. Archie Manning was a standout pro quarterback when Peyton and his brother, Eli, were growing up. One of the things about his father that impressed Peyton was that his dad came to all of their games. What Peyton noticed even more was that his father only offered words of support for him, his team and his coaches.

" 'I learned a lot from watching him as a kid,' Peyton once said. 'I learned respect for yourself, your teammates and your opponents—and respect for the game. My parents taught me early about trying to make the right choice.'

"I have fun sometimes imagining what it would be like to share a lunch table with Mother Teresa, Emerson and the Mannings. I think they share a similar approach to life in some ways. At the least, maybe they would all share this feeling: 'What was this guy *thinking* when he invited us all to lunch together?!'

"Speaking of lunch invitations, I'd like to buy you lunch sometime. Every Thursday, I eat at a place called Lenny's, a deli just south of downtown. They make a Reuben sandwich that's out of this world. I'll be there at noon. Stop by if you have the time."

After finishing the note, I glanced at my watch. It was usually the time when my daughter was taking extra shots on the backyard court. But I didn't hear the sound of her dribbling the basketball, and when I looked out the windows overlooking the court, she wasn't there. Now that I thought about it, it was the third straight day she had skipped the extra session—something she had never done previously. I was headed upstairs to check on her when she bounded down the stairs, smiling. Her smile disappeared when she saw me.

"Are you okay?" I asked.

"I'm fine," she said.

"Isn't this the time you usually practice outside? This is the third day in a row you haven't done it."

She sighed. "I know, Dad, I know. I'm swamped with school. A lot of papers and tests. I just came down to grab my history book."

"Get back on schedule tomorrow," I said, thinking I was being nice.

She turned and walked back up the steps, her head down and her shoulders slumped.

Whispering an Amen

I'm not sure why I stopped by Lenny's the next day for lunch. Maybe it was to try the Reuben. Or maybe it was to see what combination of saints, philosophers and athletes he had gathered at his table. Or maybe I felt guilty about telling him to "get the hell away from me" when he was just being nice to me and my daughter. At least part of the reason I came was because I was curious about a person who, in the only two times we met, I had been rude to—and yet he still invited me to lunch and sent me two friendly letters.

Walking inside the restaurant, I scanned the crowded, cafeteria-style line where people choose their food, but he wasn't there. So I searched for him at one of the tables. Finally, I noticed him, sitting alone at a table for two by the window, reading the newspaper. He looked up and smiled when he saw me nearing the table.

"You came!" he said, standing up and extending his right hand toward me.

"I'm surprised to see you sitting alone," I said as I shook his hand. "I thought I'd be part of a large group, including at least one of the Manning brothers."

He laughed, a deep laugh.

"No. I was just hoping you were coming," he said, beaming. "This makes my day."

I noticed he had two plates of Reuben sandwiches in front of him.

"You really do like the Reubens here," I said, smiling. "Let me get one, and I'll join you."

"One is for you," he said. "I thought with this line here, I'd just get the sandwiches and give us more time."

"So you were sure I'd come," I said.

"Like I said, just hoping. But I'm glad you're here." He motioned at the seat across from him. "Sit down. And if you don't mind, I'd like to give thanks before we eat."

He waited for me to give my permission. I nodded.

He bowed his head and said, "Thank you for the blessing of this food. And thank you for the blessing of what I hope is a new friend. Amen." He pointed to the Reuben in front of me and said, "Enjoy."

There are moments in life when you feel an immediate connection to someone you're just getting to know for the first time. I felt it when I first met my wife. Something in her eyes, her voice and the way she moved lingered in my mind, not letting me forget her, drawing me to her. When I held my daughter in the delivery room, I knew my life had changed again. Mesmerized by her, I felt an instant bond, vowing to do whatever I needed to do to care for her, protect her and make her life better in every way possible. I've had friendships in grade school, high school and college where the connections have been immediate, too. The kind of friendships where you laugh easily, trust implicitly and share the things you never tell to other people. Yet while I have been blessed to keep my connections with my wife and—until recently—with my daughter, those other friendships have faded as the years, the miles and the moves have separated us. Most of the blame is on me. So when he thanked God for the blessing of a possible new friend, something inside me stirred enough to make me silently whisper my own "Amen."

We both ate a half of our sandwiches between bits of conversation about the weather and the sports teams in our area. The Reuben was as delicious as he said it was, but before I took a bite from the second half of the sandwich, I said, "I want to apologize for the way I acted the first two times we met. Those games get to me sometimes, but that's no excuse. I'm sorry."

"Apology accepted," he said as he reached for his cup of black coffee.

"Thanks," I said. "I'm just curious about one thing. Why'd you invite me for lunch and send me those notes when I treated you like I did?"

His eyes locked on mine. It was like my daughter said: He focuses on the person he's with, making them feel like he or she is all that matters in the time he shares.

"Part of it is because of your daughter," he said. "Like I told you after that first game, I really enjoy watching her play. Then I met her in Coach Miller's office that one day. Great kid. And polite. And she looks you in the eyes. I've always liked that in a person."

He smiled as he talked about her. Then his eyes and his smile flashed a touch of mischief. "I also asked you to lunch because I wanted to meet you outside the gym—just to determine whether your daughter got all her good qualities from her mother."

I was startled at first, but then he winked, leading both of us to laugh. It was one of the traits I instantly liked about him. He often uses a touch of humor to gently chide and even disarm you, but there's never meanness in it.

"Seriously, I've been around long enough to know that your daughter is partly the way she is either because of you or in spite of you," he said. "I tend to think it's partly because of you."

For some reason, I began opening my soul to him, something I rarely do.

"When my wife was pregnant with our daughter, people often asked us if we knew the baby was a boy or a girl," I said. "We didn't want to know. We were both open to whatever we were given. People with kids would also tell us about their experiences, how boys and girls are different, and how even their relationships with their sons and daughters could be different. The one thing I constantly heard about having a girl is, 'If it's a girl, that's going to be amazing for you as a father. Having a son is special for a father, but there's *just this bond* between a dad and a daughter.' And I'd nod and think to myself, 'Sure, okay.' I still think I would have felt the same way whether we had a son or a daughter. But we had a girl, and I felt the bond right away. As she was growing up, I think she felt it, too. But now. . .I don't know. This season with basketball. . ."

My voice trailed off as I shook my head. He seemed to wait to see if I would add anything else. When I didn't, he said, "That's something I wanted to ask you about. You obviously care about your daughter or you wouldn't be there for her games. But you've looked miserable at the two games I've seen."

"She hasn't played well, and her team lost both games," I said. "That's not exactly a combination for being happy. I just want her and her team to do well."

He nodded and said, "It's hard being a parent sometimes." He paused and added, "It's hard being a son or daughter, too, sometimes. We want the best from each other. Sometimes, we want too much."

He said those words with such thoughtfulness that I didn't have the feeling he was judging me. Instead, it seemed as if he had lived the experience, one way or the other.

"By the way, I was wondering why you sit alone at the games," he said. "Doesn't your wife come to the games?"

"She'd love to," I said. "She loves watching our daughter play. But it looks like it's going to be a season when she won't be able to see her play."

"Why's that?" he asked.

"She's a high school teacher, teaches math," I started to explain. "It usually makes it easy for her to see our daughter's games. But she can't now, because she's helping out her best friend, another teacher. Her friend teaches night classes for adults wanting to get their high school diploma. But then her friend's mother had a stroke, and she asked my wife to take over her classes for a while so she could help her mom. My wife hates missing our daughter's games, but they're at the same time as the night classes. In the end, my wife decided she had to do it for her friend. That's the kind of person she is."

He nodded and said, "You married well."

"I know," I said.

I reached into my coat pocket and pulled out the two notes he had sent to me.

"I figure you've sent these notes hoping I'll ease up on my daughter," I said.

He smiled and said, "I just like to share stories with people."

We both laughed.

"Speaking of stories," he said, "I was wondering if you had one to share with me."

"What kind of story?"

"At the last game, I said there was a time when your daughter believed in you when you needed it. And I asked you to think about that moment."

"Yeah, I did," I said. "It took me a little while, but then it came to me. I just didn't know how you could know about the baseball game."

"A baseball game," he said with a smile.

"Yeah," I said. "How did you know about it?"

"I have this theory about the most important relationships in our lives," he said. "I believe there are usually special moments when the two people have shown how much they believe and trust in each other. I figured that your daughter did that for you at least once. So it happened at a baseball game. I'd like to hear you tell me the story, please."

I did. When I finished, he nodded thoughtfully and said, "That's a great story."

"Thanks," I said.

A few moments of silence passed before he said, "I guess I was right."

"About what?" I asked.

"That you do have some redeeming qualities."

We both laughed. Seconds later, I looked at my watch and realized I had to leave for a meeting.

"I have to get back to work," I said. "Thanks for inviting me. How much do I owe you for the Reuben?"

"It's my treat," he said. "But there is one favor you could do for me."

"Sure."

"Would you consider writing down the story about you and your daughter, and letting me share it with someone who could use it at some point?"

"Okay," I said.

"Great," he said. "Thanks again for coming."

I rose from my seat to leave. Standing by the table, I smiled and asked, "Should I expect to get another story soon?"

He laughed. Then he nodded and said, "Saturday."

A Child Kneels

His next letter to me naturally arrived at our house on Saturday morning. There was a brief note thanking me again for meeting him for lunch. As I would learn eventually, his notes were always just preludes to the stories. This time, they were two stories from a soccer league for 6-year-olds.

"The first story is about a boy who is more talented than most of the other players in the league," he wrote. "In fact, during one game, this boy scored four goals. And after he scored his fourth goal, he excitedly raced down the sidelines toward the place where his proud parents were standing. As he passed his parents, the boy smiled, and his parents cheered his success. Then, in a moment that some spectators will remember for a long time, the boy shouted to his parents, 'That's four bucks now! Remember, I get one dollar for each goal!'

"Now, let me share another story with you about a different child. It's a story that a father once shared with me about his son and his son's coach in that same league for 6-year-olds. In one of the games, the coach told the child to play goalie. At a certain point during the game, the action drifted to the other end of the field. That's when the goalie looked at his shoes and noticed that one of his laces had come untied. Figuring the break in the action was a good time to retie his laces, the goalie lowered to one knee to do the job.

"Now there are certain things that 6-year-olds can do quickly, such as eating cookies, asking for a new toy or suggesting that the family have pizza for dinner. But tying shoelaces isn't something that a 6-year-old does with a great deal of speed. It takes time and concentration. So as the goalie was taking his time and concentrating on his shoelaces, the action took a dramatic turn at the other end of the field. The opponents had intercepted the ball and were slowly headed in the direction of the goalie. But the boy hadn't yet noticed. He was still intently trying to tie his shoe.

"Then one of the opposing players raced past the defenders and found himself with the ball near the net. The goalie was the last person who could stop the opposing player from scoring. But there was just one small difficulty—he was still kneeling, still working on that shoelace.

"Seizing the opportunity, the opposing player kicked the ball past the goalie, his teammates cheered and only then did the goalie realize what had happened.

"Watching the incident from start to finish, the goalie's coach left the sidelines and walked toward the dejected boy. The coach didn't yell. He didn't even mention anything about the goal that had been scored. Instead, the coach knelt beside the boy and gently said, 'Let me tie your shoe for you.' Then he encouraged the boy and walked back to the sidelines.

"Two stories about children and adults. Two perspectives.

"Have a wonderful weekend. I'll see you at your daughter's game on Monday evening."

Completing the Fall from Grace

I'm always impressed by people who show grace and control under pressure, who make the right choice in a situation that could turn out badly. It's one of the reasons I love sports. In the heat of competition, sports test people mentally, physically, emotionally and even spiritually. So when I hear a story like the one about the soccer coach and the way he treated the 6-year-old boy tying his shoelaces, I realize that's the kind of person I should try to be, that I wish I could be. But I'm not. Too often, I fail in those situations, which leads me to the story of my daughter's next game, and how I stormed after her coach when the game ended.

I walked into the gym that night with the best of intentions. Looking up in the stands, I saw he was already there, munching on popcorn. The sight of him made me smile. So did his reaction when I handed him an envelope that contained the story of my daughter and me at the baseball game when she was 10.

"Thanks!" he said with his usual huge smile. "And you don't mind me sharing it with a few people?"

"No. If you think somebody would like to read it, that's fine," I said.

"Great," he said. "By the way, I got a bag of popcorn for you."

We watched the pre-game sitting next to each other, chomping on popcorn. Looking at the court, I focused on my daughter doing drills with her teammates. I couldn't believe how much she had grown up in the past few years. For some reason, I suddenly remembered a time when she was one, and I kept feeding her pieces of glazed doughnuts to keep her alive while my wife was away one weekend. I also thought of a Father's Day poem she once wrote for me, a poem in which she described me as the person "who taught me what respect was, who taught me how to believe, who worked with me for hours on my math homework, who is my guide, my role model, and at times, my best friend." I longed for those days. It was hard to believe she would be heading to college in a few years.

"You're blessed to have her in your life," he said. It was almost like he could read my mind.

"I know," I said.

I promised myself then that this game would be a turning point for me, a turning point for us. From then on, my emphasis would be on the joy with which she played and the heart she showed, instead of wins and statistics. But she didn't get to play in the game that night. Not a second.

During the game, my emotions went from expectation to hope to confusion to anger. When she didn't start, I kept expecting that she would be a substitute sometime in the first quarter. As the second quarter unfolded, I kept hoping she would enter the game soon, especially because her teammates on the court were struggling against the other team's full-court press. At halftime, I was confused.

"I don't understand why she's not playing," I said, turning to him. "She's not injured, and she looked good in the pre-game drills. And it's obvious they could use her tonight."

"Maybe the second half will be different," he said.

It was. It was far worse. With each minute that passed in the second half, the team looked more helpless and fell farther behind. With each minute that passed, I grew more agitated.

"What the hell is the coach doing?" I muttered at one point. "Why isn't he playing her?"

"Maybe there's a reason we don't know about. Coaches usually have their reasons," he said, trying to calm me.

It didn't work. In the fourth quarter, I could feel my muscles tightening and my anger growing. He noticed, too.

"Take a few deep breaths, and look at your daughter," he said. "Look at the way she's handling this."

She was on her feet in front of her team's bench, cheering for her teammates and encouraging them, even as the score became more and more lopsided.

"You have to love that attitude," he said. "*She* deserves to be cheered like that."

He stood right then and began clapping and cheering. Everyone on our side of the gym—everyone in the gym—must have thought he was crazy. There was no reason to cheer for our team. Even the parents of our girls had been silent since the first half. During the second half, all our fans just wanted the clock to wind down as quickly as possible. And now here was this lunatic standing up and cheering for no apparent reason. Only I knew the real reason, and it didn't matter to me. I flashed a death stare across the court at my daughter's coach. My daughter didn't deserve to be treated this way.

After the game finally ended and the two teams shook hands, I stomped down the wooden bleachers, across the court and along a hallway, closing in on my daughter's coach with each step as he and the team headed to the locker room. I could feel the anger surging through my body, a fury that I wanted to unleash on the coach. When I was just two steps behind the coach, I reached to grab his shoulder, but someone grabbed my shoulder first. I almost expected it to be a man holding a rolled-up bag of popcorn in his other hand. I wish it was. I might have pushed him aside. Instead, it was someone who made me stop immediately, whispering to me, "Don't do this." It was my daughter.

When I turned toward her, her eyes flashed disgust and disappointment.

She continued to whisper, "Coach asked me to get the scorebook for him, so I saw you chasing after him, looking all angry." She sighed. "You have it all wrong." She shook her head. "I need to get in there with the team. Don't even wait for me. I'll give Mom a call to pick me up."

I felt my fists unclench and my neck muscles relax. The anger drained from my body, replaced by shame and a feeling of complete loss. As I watched my daughter disappear through the locker room door, I was certain I had lost her. That's when I felt someone put a hand on my shoulder. It was him.

"Come on," he said. "Let's go some place to talk."

The Presence of Angels

We walked outside the gym and into a steady rain. Puddles had formed in the parking lot, and we dodged a few as we headed to his car. Later, I learned that he drove an old Chevy Nova because he liked that its name represented a star bursting with brightness. I also later learned that he had restored the car and painted it in a luminous, light blue color because it reminded him of a woman who had influenced his life. But I didn't pay any attention to the car that night because my mood matched the rain and the darkness, and my thoughts focused on what had just happened with my daughter.

"I can't believe I just did that," I said.

He didn't say anything as he slid the car key into the ignition.

"How much of it did you see?" I asked.

"All of it," he said. He took his right hand off the key and rested it against his right leg. "I was right beside your daughter through the crowd."

"Did she know you were there?"

"I don't think so. All her concentration was on you."

"Were you planning to stop me, too?"

"Yes, but I wanted to see what she would do first."

"I'm not sure you could have stopped me."

"It's good she did."

"Yeah."

Neither of us talked for a while. In my mind, I kept replaying the scene after the game—chasing after the coach, reaching for his shoulder, being grabbed by the shoulder by my daughter, and seeing the look in her eyes.

"Did you see the way she looked at me?" I asked.

"Yes."

"When I saw her face, I knew I was wrong to go after the coach. And it was bad enough knowing I had let myself get to that point. But then her eyes. The way she looked at me. She didn't want anything to do with me. The thing is, I know I deserve all of it."

"That's not all that was in her eyes," he said.

"What do you mean?"

"You can see her love for you. It's there, but she's hurting now, too. I think she's reached the point where she believes you just see her as 'your daughter the athlete' instead of as your daughter. I've seen that happen too many times."

The silence returned between us. As his words sank in, I looked through the windshield, watching people rush from the gym and toward their cars in the rain. A few seconds later, I saw my daughter walk slowly from the gym. Her head was down. Her hands were thrust into the pockets of her jacket. She slogged right through a few puddles before she entered my wife's car. They soon disappeared from my view.

"I hate to say it," I said, "but I can see where she could feel that way." I sighed and added, "I nearly lost her one time before, and I swore I would never let that happen again. But here we are."

"What happened the other time?" he asked.

I hesitated. It's a story I never told anyone—not even my wife. The reason I never shared the story was because I was too ashamed to let anyone else know that a short lapse on my part had almost led to losing my daughter.

I began to tell him the story.

It happened during one of our family's summer vacations. Some friends had let us use their condominium on the beach, a condominium that had a pool on the ocean side of the property, and a Jacuzzi that was even closer to the ocean. My daughter was four then, a time when her eyes usually sparkled with joy and admiration for me. She wanted to be around me, do things with me and share adventures with me. It was a time as a father when I knew what it must be like to be a hero to someone.

My wife, our daughter and I spent the morning walking on the beach, playing in the ocean and trying to build a small sand castle. I also jogged for about two miles on the beach right before lunch time. When I returned, my wife went back to the condo to get lunch ready for us. Being a little sore from everything we had done that morning, I headed toward the Jacuzzi, holding hands with my daughter as we sang some silly song she had learned in pre-school. We were all smiles as I slipped into the Jacuzzi and felt the warm whirlpool of water start to soothe my body. My daughter sat on the edge of the Jacuzzi, kicking her feet in the foamy water. Feeling the warmth of the sun and the hot rush of water, I closed my eyes. When I opened them about 30 seconds later, I looked toward where my daughter had been sitting. She wasn't there.

Bolting up, I scanned the path back to our condo. I didn't see her. A split second later, I frantically turned my eyes to the beach. I saw a girl at a similar age, with similar hair color and a similar bathing suit about 50 yards away. I almost started to run to her, but something stopped me. I turned and reached into the foamy, rushing water, right below where my daughter had been sitting on the edge of the Jacuzzi.

She was there, under the water.

I lifted her up with an urgency I never felt before. She spit out some water and gasped for a breath, finally catching it. She shook as I held her at the side of the Jacuzzi. After a while, she was breathing and acting normally. She asked me, "Daddy, why is your heart pounding, and why are you crying?"

"I'll never forget that moment when I almost ran after that other little girl," I told him. "If I had, my daughter would have. . . Fortunately, something stopped me. It was like the combination of an inner voice and a feeling telling me to check the Jacuzzi. It's hard to explain. It was like it came from inside me, but I remember feeling that it wasn't me. It was like someone else was guiding me in that moment. Like an angel."

"An angel?" he said.

"I know that sounds crazy, but. . ."

"No," he said, shaking his head. "Not to me. I've always believed in angels and the way they can help us." He paused, as if he was waiting for me to say something else. When I didn't, he said, "But it seems you're overlooking a big part of the story."

"What's that?"

"Your part," he said. "You found her and pulled her from the whirlpool. Even if you think you were guided or led by an angel, you had to act."

"What else would I do?"

"The point is, you did it. And the more I think about it, maybe that inner voice or feeling you had was just you, in a split second, figuring it all out about your daughter and the whirlpool. That she was at the edge of the pool when you last saw her. That she liked to do the things you do, and she saw you enjoying the whirlpool so she got in, too. And there was something about the other girl that made you think she was similar to your daughter, but *you knew* she wasn't your daughter. *You* put everything together and chose to check the whirlpool first."

"I don't know," I said.

"Like I said, I believe in angels. But I also believe that we're the angels sometimes, for others and ourselves."

"It's a nice thought, and I appreciate it, but I'm still the one who put her at risk."

"Okay, you made a mistake. Every parent does at some point. And most parents wish they could change at least one moment with their child. You got a chance to redeem yourself, and you did." He paused. "You could do it again."

I turned to look at him. "I'm not sure, after tonight."

"As long as there's time, there's hope," he said. "Don't give up. You haven't lost her yet."

"I hope you're right," I said. "Thanks. I'm going to head home now."

"Take care," he said.

"You, too."

I got out of his car and walked to mine. The rain had stopped. The sky was clearing. When I got home, neither my wife nor my daughter was still awake. Passing by my daughter's room, I opened the door and peaked inside. Her study light was still on, and an open textbook was right beside the light, but she was asleep in her bed. I tiptoed across the cream-colored carpet and started to turn off the light. Instead, I stopped and looked at her. When my daughter was little, I always kissed her forehead at bedtime, said, "God bless you," and told her, "I love you." She always responded, "I love you, too." As she got older, I kept the same ritual, but she responded with a single word, "likewise." I knew it was a sign that she was changing, but it still meant a lot to me to know the connection was still there. Standing by her bed at that moment, I thought about how that ritual had disappeared between us in the past year. I also thought about how he said there was still hope. I leaned over, kissed her on the forehead, and whispered, "God bless you. I love you." I clicked off the study light and left her room.

Trusting in the Unknown

He surprised me the following afternoon when he sent his next story. It was the first time I received one of his stories by e-mail. The story also surprised me because it focused on an activity that many people don't naturally think of as a sport.

"One of the most horrifying and inspiring stories I've ever heard involves a skydiver named Roger Reynolds," he began. "He was a member of the Army's Golden Knights skydiving team. For two years, he awed crowds with his stunts. He had also made 959 successful jumps up to that point in his life. Full of confidence, he prepared to make his 960th jump in front of the 6,000 people who had come to the air show on that cold, gloomy day. As the plane soared to 2,000 feet, Reynolds moved to the edge of the open door. He scanned the sky beneath him. Then he jumped. Floating through the air, he knew the exact moment when he wanted to pull his parachute. Yet when he did, it didn't open. Still, he felt no panic. He reached for his backup parachute. He pulled again. It didn't open either. The world and his life rushed by as he fell 2,000 feet and slammed into the ground.

"They found his crumpled body on the soft ground of a doctor's backyard, just a few feet from a concrete driveway. Blood was everywhere. Nearly every bone in his body was broken. But Reynolds was alive.

"His hospital stay was a long one, and his recovery took three years. People thought he would never want to jump again. Reynolds had his doubts, too. But eventually, he did. In fact, he continued skydiving long enough to try to make his 2,000th jump. That day was as cold and dreary as the day he jumped and nearly died. The weather conditions also forced him to jump from 2,000 feet, the same height he jumped from when his two parachutes didn't open. This time, with no crowd there to cheer him, he landed safely.

"When newspapers later celebrated him for his 2,000th jump, I found myself instead thinking about Reynolds on his 961st jump, the first one he made after his near-fatal accident. No one would have ever blamed him if he had never skydived again. But Reynolds didn't want that 960th jump to be the way that part of his life story ended. I imagined him moving to the edge of the plane's open door. I also envisioned him looking down, all the time knowing that the last time he jumped he nearly died. Amazingly, he still jumped—leaping into the unknown, trusting in himself, and believing that the result would be positive. What a great way to live."

When I finished the story, I thought about the "leap" that I had already decided to make later that day. Before his story about Reynolds arrived, I wasn't sure how that leap would turn out or if I would change my mind at the last second and not take it. There was no way he could have known about the leap I was considering. Could he? Still, he suddenly gave me the extra confidence to take it.

A Leap of Faith

After work that day, I drove to my daughter's school. My wife had already told me that she would pick up our daughter after practice, that our daughter was still upset with me from last night. So I wasn't going to the school to take her home. I was headed there to talk to her coach.

I arrived 20 minutes after I knew practice was scheduled to end, a time when I knew the girls had already left, and Coach Miller was usually still in his office. As I walked along the hall to his office, he was just coming out of it when he noticed me. He smiled, greeted me by name and told me that my daughter had just left with my wife.

"I know," I said. "I wanted to talk to you. To see if I could set up a time to talk with you."

Those words—or a variation of them—from a parent must trigger an alarm in the minds of most coaches, setting off the unsettling feeling that here's another parent with a complaint. Coach

Miller showed some of the immediate physical reactions to those words, too. His shoulders slumped. His smile disappeared. Still, he composed himself and asked, "What would you like to talk about?"

"Last night's game," I said.

He nodded, seemed to think about something, and said, "If you want to talk now, this is as good a time as any for me."

"Sure," I said.

We walked into his office. He sat behind his desk while I slipped into the seat in front of him. What I said in the next few minutes stunned him. It also would have shocked anyone who noticed the way I reacted during last night's game and after it. In fact, I surprised myself, too.

"I want to apologize to you," I began. Then I told him how I reacted to my daughter not playing during the game, and how I chased him after the game until my daughter stopped me.

"When she did, I knew I was wrong," I told him. "I should have listened to my friend who was sitting next to me during the game. He told me that coaches usually have a reason for the decisions they make, and you probably had one for not playing my daughter last night. I should have asked her about it first, but that time has passed. And she's not exactly in a mood right now to talk with me. Besides, I'm not here to ask you about your reason either. I just came here to apologize to you. It just seems that it's one of the things I have to do if I'm going to start to make things right somehow with my daughter. I'm sorry for how I acted."

I put my hands on the arm rests of my chair. "I'm going to leave now," I said. "Thanks for your time, Coach."

He looked stunned as I left his office. I began walking down the hall until I heard Coach Miller calling me from behind, standing outside his office. He said he wanted to talk to me.

As we sat again in his office, I listened this time. What he eventually told me stunned me as much as I had initially stunned him.

"First, I want to thank you for coming in and talking to me," he said. "I rarely get parents dropping by and apologizing for anything, let alone something you didn't even do." He smiled. "But if you think it's one of the steps you need to take to help you set things straight with your daughter, I'm glad you did it."

He leaned forward in his chair, put his arms on the desk and folded his hands.

"Now, there *was* a good reason for why I didn't play your daughter last night. She really didn't want me to tell anybody about it, but considering that you're trying to make things right with her and considering something else that happened today, I think you should know the reason.

"She came in here three days ago to talk to me. She told me she was going to quit the team, that she wasn't having fun anymore. I asked her what the problem was, if we were doing anything from a coaching standpoint that made her feel that way. Or if there was something I could do to change her mind. She said it wasn't the team or the coaches, it was something else. But she wouldn't elaborate."

By now, Coach Miller knew that the most likely reason for her to consider quitting was sitting right across the desk from him. Yet, much to his credit, he didn't stop talking and look at me as if I was guilty. He just continued.

"Now when most girls say they're going to quit, they've already made up their minds, and there's nothing you can do to change them," he said. "But I wanted to give her the opportunity to think it over, especially considering the way she plays the game and the way she is with her teammates. So I asked her to just watch last night's game from the bench, to see what it would be like if she wasn't playing. To see if she would miss it. I can't tell you how hard that was for me, especially with how we were struggling last night. And I know how hard it was for her—and her teammates, too. But I think it made her see how much she wanted to play, not just for herself but for her teammates. It was great the way she kept cheering for them until the end. And today, she came into my office before practice. She told me she wanted to keep playing, and she was sorry for almost quitting. That was a great win for me. She had a great practice. *We* had a great practice. It's been the kind of day that reminds me what I love about coaching."

As he smiled, I lowered my head.

"I can't believe I almost ruined it for her," I said. "Sports are one of the things that made us close, at least until this season."

"The good news is she's still playing, and you want to make things right with her," he said. "Like I always tell the girls, the last play is in the past. Learn from it, and focus on the next play."

"You sound like my friend," I said.

"Must be a good friend," he said. "Who is he?"

"I've been sitting at the past few games with him. Older guy. Wears white, high-top Chuck Taylor sneakers. His friends have an unusual nickname for him. . ."

"God?!" he asked with a smile.

"You call him that, too?" I said.

"Very rarely," he said.

"How do you know him?"

"It was years ago, in my first couple of years of coaching," he said. "Back then, it was all about winning for me. I thought the wins and losses personally reflected on me. I'd yell at the kids, yell at the refs. I yelled at him several times. Then I'd go back after the game and look at the plays where I knew he made the wrong call, and it turned out he was right. One time, I went into this place for lunch, and he was sitting there alone, eating. I went over, and he invited me to sit down. We became friends. Found out he knows everything about basketball. Found out he knows even more about people. He taught me to put people before the game. I hadn't seen him in about ten years. Then he showed up at one of our games earlier this season and came into my office the next day. Wearing those white high-tops. Looking the same as he did. And that voice. I thought he was checking up on me." He smiled at me. "I guess he's concentrating on you."

"It seems that way," I said sheepishly.

"By the way, I've asked him to share some stories with the girls," Coach Miller said. "He said he would. His plan is for the girls to get them every once in a while throughout the rest of the season."

Before I left his office, I asked Coach Miller for a favor.

"If you don't mind, don't mention to my daughter that I stopped by today," I said. "I don't want her to get the wrong idea about why I came here to see you. And maybe it's best that she thinks that only you and she know she was considering quitting. Still, I really appreciate you telling me."

As we shook hands, I knew my toughest apology was next.

Chasing a Rebound

When I steered my car into our driveway that evening, I saw my daughter shooting, rebounding and smiling for the first time in weeks. I also saw her smile disappear when I walked onto the court and grabbed the ball as it headed in my direction after a missed shot.

"I don't need your help," she said icily.

"I know," I said, holding the ball. "I just want to apologize for last night—and the way I've been at other times this season. And I want to thank you for saving me from..."

She cut me off and said, "Could I just have the ball back, please? I want to get my shots in before I help Mom with dinner and have to start studying."

"Sure," I said. I passed the ball back to her, walked off the court and toward the house where I saw my wife standing by the opened back door. She had heard our conversation.

"Thanks for trying to apologize to her," my wife said as we walked inside together.

"She wasn't having any part of it," I said. "Not that I blame her."

"She was really upset last night when she got into the car. She said she wishes you wouldn't come to any more of her games."

I felt my shoulders slump and my heart sink.

"I guess I can understand that, especially since she was ready to quit the team because of me. Did you know that?"

"Not until last night," she said. "On the way home, she told me she had been considering it. But she said watching last night's game made her realize how much she loves the game and her teammates."

"That's good to hear," I said. "At least I didn't take that away from her."

"Look, there's no doubt you have to get better about keeping her sports in perspective. But you also have to realize she's growing up. She's not our little girl anymore."

"I thought she was always supposed to be our little girl," I said with a half-smile.

"Okay, I won't completely ruin your dad-daughter fantasy," she said, smiling. Then she turned serious. "Just know that there are going to be a few years—and they're coming soon—when you're not going to be a major factor in her life. Just ask my dad about my senior year in high school and my college years. So trust me on this: If you keep doing things that push her away, she's not just going to grow up, she's going to grow away from you even quicker and for longer. And I know you don't want that to happen."

Just then, the back door opened, and our daughter walked through it, holding the basketball.

"Perfect timing," my wife said, switching conversations smoothly. "After you wash your hands, I could use help with the salad."

"Thanks for the talk," I told my wife as our daughter washed her hands in the bathroom. "I definitely married out of my league."

"Yes, you did," she said with a smile. "Most men do."

Almost Everything You Really Need to Know About Life You Could Learn in a Gym

On the issue of whether or not to snoop into their child's life, many parents consider it perfectly acceptable to do so. These parents view it as a way to understand what's really happening in a child's life, and maybe even save the child from making or continuing an ill-advised or even dangerous choice. Other parents believe that their relationship with a child has to rest on a foundation of respect and trust, and snooping undermines that foundation. Then there are the parents who embrace the ideal of respect and trust in their relationships with their child, yet sometimes get led astray from it when they come across something that catches their attention or curiosity. I'm a charter member of the third group. And my tendency to snoop usually increases during times when my daughter shuts me out of her life. For the second straight day, she didn't talk to me when I came home from work.

So my curiosity prevailed when I saw the opened envelope on the top of my daughter's gym bag that evening. By the handwriting on the outside of the envelope, I knew it had come from the same source as all the letters I had already received this season. I figured that the note inside must be the first of the stories that he was sending to the players on my daughter's team, just as Coach Miller had asked him to do. Considering the variety of stories he had shared with me, I wondered what stories he would share with them. After I made sure that my daughter was still practicing outside, I took the note from the envelope. But it wasn't a story. It was a list: "Almost Everything You Really Need to Know about Life, You Could Learn in a Gym." Here it is.

Work together.

Keep your head up.

What you do on your own when no one is watching will determine how good you will become.

The best person on a team is the one who strives to make everyone around him or her better.

Play with heart.

Don't be afraid to take your shot.

Never let your view of your value be determined by other people's cheers, boos or opinions.

You should never ask people the name of their eye doctor while they are officiating a basketball game. Trust me.

Stay under control.

Never back down from a challenge.

People will taunt you, criticize you, and question your ability. Respond with hard work, not harsh words.

The price of a person's shoes never shows the value of the person wearing them.

Be unselfish.

Focus on what you need to do.

Thank the people who always support you.

Thank the people who take the time to teach you.

Set goals.

Pursue your dream.

Treat everyone with respect, including your opponents.

When the breaks go against you, don't quit or complain. Try to overcome them.

Winners and losers pay the same price for pizza after the game. It's a different way of saying that in the larger world most people don't care about your successes and failures.

But don't let that ever stop you from caring.

Everyone has bad days.

Show your class in the tough times.

Show your humility in the good times.

Winning at all costs is a price too steep to pay.

People on your team won't remember you for how often you succeeded as much as they'll remember you for how you treated them.

And one more thing: Have some fun today.

The Lesson That All Great Teammates Learn

"Do you know what it takes to be a great teammate?"

That question started the second note that he wrote to my daughter and her teammates, a note that I found open on top of my daughter's sports bag the next day.

"For me, there are two qualities that make for a great teammate," he continued. "Today, I'd like to focus on one of those qualities by telling you the story of two players with dreams. The first player was Walter Payton, one of the greatest running backs in the history of the National Football League. At the time of this story, he had achieved nearly everything in his career—records and All-Pro honors—but his dream of winning the Super Bowl had eluded him. The second player was named Kevin Kelly, a recent high school graduate at the time who wanted to play football in college.

"On a late Friday night that year, Kelly had just left his part-time factory job when he walked into a 24-hour health club near his suburban Chicago home. He wanted to work on increasing his strength—an area he knew he needed to improve to play in college. When he entered the weight room, only one other person was there, a man that Kelly recognized immediately—Payton, the star running back of the Chicago Bears who was one of Kelly's idols. Figuring that Payton had chosen this late hour to train alone, Kelly didn't say a word, but he stayed to lift weights. A few minutes later, Payton walked across the room and asked Kelly to work out with him. They ended their session nearly four hours later. Before they left the gym, Payton gave Kelly his phone number and told him to call him the next day so they could train together again.

"After they had trained together for two weeks, Payton phoned Kelly one day to ask if he wanted to run 'The Hill' with him. Kelly said sure, believing that The Hill was just a small grade of land with a gentle slope. Yet when they stood at the bottom of The Hill, Kelly couldn't believe it. The Hill looked more like a mountain. It was 70 yards high and had a slope with a 45-degree angle. To run up it even once, Kelly thought, was to punish your body. Standing there, Payton said they would run The Hill at least 10 times and 20 times if possible. Between each run, Payton added, they would rest for 30 seconds. Kelly thought Payton was crazy. But he matched him.

"That summer, the All-Pro running back and the soon-to-be college student ran The Hill and lifted weights seven days a week. When Kelly left for college, Payton told him to stay in touch. Kelly thought it was a nice gesture on Payton's part, but he didn't think their friendship would continue once the Bears' season began. He didn't call Payton. So one day, Payton called

The Lesson That All Great Teammates Learn | 59

him. He told Kelly that it didn't matter where he was, that they were still friends.

"Their friendship continued. When Kelly came home for summers, he and Payton returned to lifting weights and running The Hill together. And they stayed in touch throughout the rest of the year, talking on the phone a few times a week. Sometimes, Kelly told Payton about trying to earn a starting position on his college team while Payton told Kelly about playing with the Bears. Still, Kelly never expected what Payton did in the weeks leading up to the Bears playing in the Super Bowl for the first time in Payton's career. During an interview with Payton, reporters wanted to know what pushed him a step further in his quest for a championship. As part of his answer, Payton mentioned Kelly, saying, 'He never quits. He never wants anybody to outdo him.'

"When those words appeared in print, Kelly was surprised. He thanked Payton. But Payton said the public compliment was long overdue, and it was just his way of sharing the spotlight with someone who made him a better person and a better athlete. Later, Kelly shared his view of Payton, saying, 'I have a tremendous amount of respect for him. You see a lot of guys with great athletic ability, but what really sets him apart is his will and his drive. I'm even more impressed by the person he is. He's taught me a lot of things. He's like a brother to me. When I was in high school, there was no doubt he was a hero to me. Now, we're friends. I think it just says a lot that he appreciates another person for what they are.'

"The Bears won the Super Bowl that year, and Payton crowned his outstanding career with a championship. It was one more reason to celebrate Payton. Yet so are the words that Kelly used to describe him: 'He appreciates another person for what they are.' That's the first quality of a great teammate. At some point, all teammates meet as strangers. They come to a team with their own hopes, fears and dreams. In the end, though, the best teammates are the ones who make a commitment to each other as people first. Payton and Kelly lived that quality as teammates. They understood the lesson that all great teammates eventually learn: When you care about each other as people, and when you respect each other's contributions and dreams, you make connections that bind you forever."

Reaching for a Dream

He shared the second quality of a great teammate in the note he gave to my daughter and her teammates a day later. As I read it while my daughter practiced outside, I could picture him laughing at himself when he wrote the first sentence of the note.

"No doubt, you've been waiting breathlessly since yesterday for me to tell you about the other important quality in being a special teammate. Once again, it seems that the best way to share that quality with you is through a story. This one comes from a basketball coach named Al Sokaitis. He told the story as he talked to more than 1,500 youths during a Final Four basketball clinic one year. He began by asking the audience, 'How many people have laid in bed at night and made the shot that won the state championship?'

"When nearly every hand in the gym shot into the air, Sokaitis said, 'Let me tell you about that shot. I don't want my players to be dreamers at night. I want my players to be dreamers during the day. I want them to practice and prepare for making that shot.'

"Then he told a humorous and telling story from the days he coached a high school team that was in the state championship game. The game was in its final seconds, and one of his players was getting ready to shoot a foul shot that could win the game. As the player waited for the ball from the referee, a teammate shouted to him, 'Nets for a soda.' The player at the foul line nodded and smiled.

"An outsider would have wondered if the tension of that moment had overwhelmed the two teammates. But they knew that 'Nets' was a game they had played during every practice. Sokaitis used the game to have his players improve their foul-shooting. A player received a point each time a successful foul shot touched nothing but the net. So in the crucial moment of a crucial game, one teammate was challenging another to swish the foul shot—for a soda.

"When the player shot the ball, it glanced slightly against the rim before it went in, sending Sokaitis and his team's 9,000 fans at the game into complete ecstasy. So what word did the shooter use to express his emotions for the biggest shot of his life? He said, 'Dang.' He was mildly upset that he hadn't swished the shot, knowing it cost him a soda.

"Sokaitis swore it was a true story. He told the youths in the audience, 'You've got to make practice tougher than the game. If you want to be good at something, all you have to do is reach for it. But you got to reach for it.'

"So there you have the second quality of a great teammate—making the commitment to each other to get better every day. Combine that quality with the commitment to care for and respect your teammates as people, and great experiences and lasting relationships should come your way."

Riding High, Lying Low

There's no way to know for sure what impact, if any, his first three notes had on my daughter and her teammates. Yet it was obvious that something had changed dramatically for her and her team during the first half of their next game. They scored the first ten points of the game against a team that had won five in a row. By halftime, their lead had grown to 15 points. Everyone looked relaxed and confident, including my daughter who made six of the seven shots she took in the first half. She hadn't shot this well in a long time during a game, but her shooting wasn't the biggest difference I noticed in her. Most of all, she looked *happy*—far happier than I had seen her since the season began. I tried not to think too much of the fact that her increased happiness came during a time when she was mostly distant and cool toward me. It was easier to overlook that fact because of the fun she and her teammates were having on the court.

I watched that game from the most out-of-the-way place in the gym. I sat in the last row, on our side of the gym, in the upper left-hand corner. I chose that location because I remembered my daughter had told my wife that she wished I would stay away from her games. Considering that my daughter hadn't shared that wish directly with me—she had barely talked to me since the night I went after Coach Miller—I decided I would continue to come to the games but sit in a place where I wasn't noticeable to her. I didn't think anyone would find me there until I saw a pair of white, high-top Chuck Taylor sneakers bounding up the wooden bleachers, heading right toward me before the game. I had been winded from making that climb. He looked fresh when he reached the last row.

"Did you get reduced admission for this seat or have you entered the Witness Protection Program?" he said with a smile. "If I didn't have such good eyesight, I'm not sure I would have noticed you from court level."

I explained the reason for my seat choice.

His face turned serious, and he nodded. "Sometimes, lying low is a good way to go," he said.

"Yeah, but it's not fun being the bad guy," I said. "At the same time, I know I only have myself to blame for being in this position."

"Being the bad guy sometimes serves a good purpose, too," he said. "Even as a parent. Right now, it seems she's pushing back at you. But the good part is she's also taking control of her situation, doing things on her own terms. That's a good development, even if it's just a reaction against you right now."

"I see that," I said. "I just wish I wasn't living it."

"Hang in there," he said. "The game isn't over."

The game on the court began a few moments later. Midway through the first quarter, he looked over at me and said, "Wow!"—

reacting to the way my daughter and her teammates were playing. Time after time, he rose and cheered during that stretch, showing his appreciation for every hustle play, every defensive stop and every beautiful assist. He stood and cheered so routinely that, by the end of the first quarter, he told me he had to move to another part of the gym.

"If they keep playing this way, and if I keep standing and cheering, I'll eventually draw attention to us, if I haven't already," he said. "With you trying to lie low, I need to move because I can't stop cheering for this kind of effort."

"Thanks," I said.

The team continued playing at that high level throughout the game, and he continued standing and cheering. I have to admit there were a few times in the second half when I jumped from my seat and cheered, too, forgetting my goal to go unnoticed. But then I sat down quickly and lowered my head. I also have to admit that I recognized the difference in the times when he and I cheered. I cheered when we scored. He sometimes cheered when we made a shot, but he always saved his loudest and most enthusiastic cheers for those moments when a player displayed extra effort or did the small, selfless things that were rarely noticed by most fans, such as setting a solid screen, helping out on defense and encouraging teammates from the bench. Either way, there were plenty of reasons to cheer the team that day. By the end of the game—a convincing win—I was so pumped with joy that I unconsciously started to walk down the bleachers, wanting to congratulate and share the moment with my daughter. He cut me off, before I had taken three steps.

"What a game!" he said.

"Unbelievable," I said. "I was just going to tell my daughter that."

He put his right hand on my left shoulder. "You can't," he said.

"I always do after she plays well and her team wins," I said.

"Not today," he said.

"Why not?" I said.

"Remember, you thought it was best to lie low for a while at her games," he said. "So do I. Trust me on this. Be patient."

I knew he was right. I sat down. He joined me, telling me how much he loved to watch my daughter play. As he talked, I looked down on the court where my daughter shared laughs and smiles with her teammates, and received compliments and hugs from other parents. At one point, for the briefest of moments, I thought I saw her look up in the direction of where we were seated. I thought she was even headed toward us, but she quickly turned away as if she hadn't seen us. I guess it was just my imagination—or my hope.

What It Means to Matter in the Life of a Child

He hadn't sent me a note in more than a week. When the next one arrived, it was a bit of a surprise, especially considering the story he shared—the story of a part-time professional wrestler named Doctor Doom.

"Before the last game, we talked about how being the bad guy sometimes serves a good purpose. Just to let you know that you're not alone, I'd like to introduce you to Doctor Doom, one of the most dastardly villains in professional wrestling. He earned his nickname by putting opponents 'to sleep' through some questionable tactics and secret weapons that he used when he blocked the ref's view. He always looked menacing in black knee-high boots, black-and-red-striped shirt, and a black hood trimmed in blood-red. Wrestling fans loved to boo him lustily. And he savored every boo.

"But wrestling was always just a part-time gig. By day, he is a real medical doctor by the name of Dr. Chuck Dietzen, although most people just call him 'Doctor Chuck.' Doctor Chuck once told me that in matters of hope and healing, he believes that God is always present, but that God usually makes his presence known in the form of another human being. I've always liked that thought, and I've always liked him. He has dedicated his medical career to caring for children, with a special emphasis on kids with spinal injuries, head injuries and other disabilities. One of those children was a boy named Jacob who had a blood clot form in his brain. After Jacob was rushed to the hospital, doctors tried to prepare his parents for the likelihood that their son would soon die. Even when Jacob beat the odds, his future seemed to offer little promise. The boy couldn't eat, swallow, talk or move when he arrived at the specialty hospital where children come for therapy and rehabilitation.

"Doctor Chuck worked there at the time. After two days at the hospital, Jacob wasn't showing any signs of improvement. His mother sat beside his bed, praying for him, feeling hopeless. Doctor Chuck came into the room for the first time. He answered her questions and tried to soothe her fears. Recalling that first meeting with Doctor Chuck, Jacob's mother said, 'He gave me such hope. And that was something no one else had given me.' When several months had passed, Jacob could eat, swallow and talk. Best of all to his mother, he could give her hugs.

"While a mother needs to hear hope for her children and receive hugs from her children, children need certain things, too. Children need to believe in themselves. Children also need to believe they can overcome obstacles and setbacks to do great things in their lives. Doctor Chuck understands those needs of children. He also knows that children love to be active, especially kids whose physical movements are limited by injury or circumstances of birth. That's why he scheduled a wrestling match pitting the dastardly Doctor Doom against Jake the Snake, a then-nine-year-old boy who looked exactly like Jacob. In fact, he was Jacob.

"A wrestling ring was set up in the hospital. A crowd rimmed the ring. When Doctor Doom jumped into the ring, in full costume and full scowl, the fans booed. Then they stood and cheered when Jake the Snake arrived, flexing his muscles. Everyone viewed it as a classic battle between good and evil. In the end, good prevailed. Jake the Snake pinned Doctor Doom. Jake the Snake flashed a huge smile and raised his arms in triumph as the defeated Doctor Doom handed over his championship wrestling belts. It was a moment that Jacob's mother will never forget.

"Minutes after the wrestling match, Doctor Doom walked back to his locker room, which also happened to be Doctor Chuck's office. On the way, he passed a framed picture of a boy standing on a beach, looking out to the sea. The text at the bottom of the picture noted, 'A hundred years from now, it will not matter what my bank account was, the sort of house I lived in, or the kind of car I drove...but the world may be different because I was important in the life of a child.'

"You're in good company as a bad guy."

Making the Right Call

One of my favorite stories that I heard during that season wasn't from him. It was about him. As much as he loved to tell stories, he never told me one about himself. This story came from Dan, the guy who had been on the same crew of refs with him for a few years. Dan told me the story when we ran into each other one Saturday morning at the grocery store, in the produce section. I was picking up a bunch of bananas when he greeted me with a mischievous smile and the kind of sarcastic yet good-natured question that is sometimes asked by guys who are friends.

"So how's the guy who told 'God' to get the hell away from him doing these days?" Dan asked, grinning.

We both laughed.

"He told me that your daughter's team has won a few games in a row, and she's playing well," he said.

"Yeah, it's been a fun stretch," I said. "So do you talk to him a lot?"

"Just now and then," Dan said. "Not enough. I've been trying to stay in touch after talking to him at that game at the beginning of the season. I don't know why I haven't done a better job because I always feel good after talking to him. And I love to hear his stories."

"He always seems to have one ready," I said with a smile. I paused before asking, "Do you have any stories about him?"

"What kind of stories?"

"Anything," I said. "It just hit me right now that he's told me a lot of stories, too, but they've never been about him. I just thought you might have a story about him—from working with him."

"I do have one favorite story about him," Dan said. "It was the last time we worked a game together. I think it was the last time he worked as a ref, too. But for the story to have its full impact, it helps to know his approach as a ref, and what I learned from him. He never shied away from making the tough call, even when the game was in the balance. Still, his ultimate goal was to make each game as fair and as good as possible for the players in it. And he kept stressing that we couldn't let anything get in the way of that goal. There was one game where a coach objected to nearly every call I made, so I just kept calling foul after foul on his team to show him I was in control. But the truth is, I had lost control. I was so focused on making a point that the coach wasn't going to show me up that I wasn't fair to the players on his team. When I sat in the locker room after the game and cooled down, I knew I had let my ego get in the way of calling the game. He knew it, too. But he didn't say it. He asked me what I thought about the game. I told him. He sat down across from me and said, 'We're all human. We make mistakes. Learn from it, and do better the next time.' The usual stuff. Then he added something that has stayed with me, 'If you're going to show your human side during the game, err on the good side of your humanity.'

"I tell you all this because it sets the background for the last game he worked as a ref. It happened during the championship game of a freshmen girls' high school basketball tournament. It was just the two of us working the game. Both teams played terrific. In fact, one team went ahead by hitting a shot with 10 seconds left in regulation, and the other team hit a shot at the buzzer to send it into overtime. That play also ended my afternoon. Running from one end of the court to the other, I heard a pop in my right knee and collapsed at half-court. A trainer, the two coaches, 'God' and my wife—who was in the stands to support me—rushed to help me. They eventually got me to my feet, but I couldn't walk. My wife wanted to take me to the hospital right then, but I wanted to see the end of the game. So I leaned against her, watching with a bag of ice on my knee and a pair of crutches nearby.

"He worked the rest of the game alone. And he did a hell of a job, especially considering the game went into four overtimes. It was the most amazing game I've ever seen. Remember how one team tied the game at the buzzer in regulation? Well, the other one returned the favor at the end of the first overtime. And then they took turns doing the same thing at the end of the second and third overtimes. But something even more amazing happened by then. Earlier in the game, some players had been trash talking, and a lot of the fans and coaches were yelling and questioning calls—at least my calls. But with every passing minute of the four overtimes, the attitudes of everyone in the gym kept changing for the better. I think some of it was because everyone was emotionally drained and physically exhausted from playing and even watching the game. And some of it was just pure mutual respect for the efforts of the girls on both teams. I even think there was genuine appreciation from everyone for the one ref out there, working his tail off.

"At the end of the fourth overtime, there was no last-second shot to end the game, which was again tied. 'God' walked slowly to the sidelines during the break. His face was deep red, and his ref's shirt was soaked with sweat. He stopped at both teams' benches and asked the two coaches to meet him at the scorer's table. I listened as he told them, 'I'm sorry. I can't go on. I'm afraid my heart won't take it if we go another overtime.' He slumped against the scorer's table. The athletic director wanted to call an ambulance, but he said he just wanted to rest. When he sat down, my wife, a nurse, took his vital signs. She told him then—and me later—that they were surprisingly good. He just sat on the bench, looking at the players and the coaches, almost like he wanted to see what would happen next.

"What did happen next was something I had never seen before or since. While the athletic director tried to get in touch with other refs by phone, the two coaches asked their fans if anyone had experience as a referee. That's when I saw a girl from each of the teams talking at half-court. They smiled at each other as they walked away and began talking with their teammates. Looking from one group to another, I could see every head in each group nodding in agreement. The two girls then met at half-court again, with the rest of their teammates following closely. The two girls talked again, and smiled even more this time. They then asked both of their coaches to meet with them.

"The girls had decided that even if another ref could be found, they weren't going to play anymore. They told their coaches they had given everything they could. They thought it would be great if they could be considered co-champions. But even if neither one of them were declared champions or co-champions, they said that was fine with them. They just didn't think it was right if one of the teams lost. Both coaches looked at each other. One extended her hand. The other shook it. The two teams gathered around each other. A few minutes later, they were all in the middle of the court together, standing in front of the championship trophy as their parents and grandparents snapped the photo from every angle.

"At that moment, I saw what I think only my wife and I noticed. I saw 'God' stand and smile. A few minutes later, he helped my wife help me into our car so she could drive me to the hospital. I told him he should come with us, to get his heart checked. But he said he felt better. As he patted me on the shoulder, I asked him, 'Are you sure your heart is fine?' He winked and said, 'It wouldn't have been if I had to see one of those teams lose today. Don't worry about me. I'm good. Let me know what the doctors say about your knee.' I nodded and asked him another question, 'What did you think of the choice the girls made?' He smiled. Then he said, 'It was what I was hoping for. I can't think of a better ending for that game.'

"He was right. It was the best game I was ever part of."

Surprising Moves

Two days later, he was already waiting for me in the far corner of the gym where I had tried to go unnoticed by my daughter for the last three games. As I reached the halfway point of the long climb, he stood and mouthed the musical theme from the original *Rocky* movie, the theme that built to a crescendo when Rocky—the ultimate underdog boxer—ran up the steps of Philadelphia's art museum while training for a fight. I humored him by raising my arms and pumping them into the air as I ran up the last five rows of bleachers to where he stood.

"You're looking strong, Rock," he said, perfectly mimicking the gravelly voice of Mick, Rocky's trainer in the movie, as he handed me a bottle of water.

"Thanks, Mick," I said, accepting the water.

We had reached a new point in our friendship. On one level, it was a point where we could easily clown with each other. On another level, it was also a point where I felt comfortable in openly complimenting him. That part of a friendship, especially with other men, had always been the hardest for me. But it had become natural with him.

"By the way, I ran into Dan the other day, and he said to tell you hello," I said.

"Thanks. How's he doing?"

"He's good," I said. "He was in rare form, telling me this great story about you and him from the days you were refs together."

"Which story?" he asked.

Down on the court, the two teams ran onto the floor for pre-game warm-ups. The scoreboard began to count down the twenty minutes to the start of the game.

"The four-overtime game," I said as I watched my daughter drive to the basket during the lay-up drill.

"What a terrific game," he said.

"The way Dan told the story made me wonder. There wasn't actually anything physically wrong with your heart, was there?"

"Are you questioning a ref's call?"

"It's the first time I've ever done that," I said with a smile.

"Now, that's hard to believe," he said.

We both laughed.

"Here's what I'll tell you," he said. "Near the end of the fourth overtime, there was a play where a girl drove to the basket, and a girl on the other team set up in the lane to defend the drive. They both ended up on the floor in one of those moments where one side thinks it's a blocking foul on the defensive player, and the other side believes it's a charging foul on the offensive player. Being the only ref on the court, I wasn't in a good position to make the call. So I swallowed my whistle. I didn't call a foul either way. I expected both girls, both coaches and both sets of fans to be upset. Instead, both girls helped each other up from the floor and didn't say a word to me. I know you had to be there to believe it, but that's the way most of that game was played. And after that play, I knew I didn't want to see either team lose. It's like I told Dan in the parking lot that day. My heart wouldn't have been fine if I had to see one of those teams lose that game. So there was a heart concern for me. And it got much better when the girls did what they did." He paused and added, "It's the only time I ever did that as a ref. Sometimes, you just have to go against the usual, expected way of doing things—because you know it's *the right thing* to do or it will hopefully lead to the right result."

"For what it's worth, I think you made a good call," I said.

"Thanks," he said. "I'm just a little surprised to hear you say that."

"Why?" I asked.

"Your natural tendency is to see things in black and white. Points on the scoreboard. Wins and losses," he said. "And I'm not being critical of that approach. I understand it. A lot of people would disagree with me if they knew what I did. So I appreciate your support." He paused and asked, "Are there any one-of-a-kind moments when you've gone against your usual, expected way of doing things?"

I looked down to the court to find my daughter. I saw her stretching with some of her teammates, doing one of the stretches she learned from her earlier years as a dancer.

"Not anything on the level that you did," I said.

"But something?" he asked.

"Yeah, although it had nothing to do with sports," I said.

"What was it?" he asked.

"I took dancing lessons once," I said sheepishly.

He laughed.

"If you saw me dance, you'd be laughing even harder," I said.

"I'm sorry," he said, smiling. "I was just picturing you taking lessons. Why did you take them?"

"When my daughter was in the sixth grade, they learned different dances as part of their gym class," I said. "One of the dances the sixth-grade boys and girls learned was the waltz. As part of a school program one night, the sixth-grade boys were supposed to dance the waltz with their moms, and the sixth-grade girls would dance with their dads. I cringed when I heard about it. I don't like to dance. Mainly because I've always been a *really* lousy dancer. But I wanted to learn the steps to the waltz because my daughter knew them, and I wanted to do them right for her. So I took dance lessons at a local studio. It wasn't pretty. In fact, when I finished my last lesson, the poor woman who taught me all five times told me she would pray for me on the night of the program. But I think I did a decent job because my daughter looked up and smiled at me at the end of the dance."

"No doubt she appreciated that you took lessons for her," he said.

"I never told her about them," I said. "I just wanted her to remember it as a special moment with her dad."

Looking at the Game in a Different Way

Right before the game started that day, he followed his recent routine of moving to a different section of the gym so his cheering wouldn't bring any attention to me. It was just one of the patterns that had continued throughout the past four games. During that stretch, I hid in the farthest reaches of the gym during games, my daughter stayed polite but distant toward me during our interactions at home, and she and her teammates played at a level that was a joy to watch. Considering that all four games had been wins, there didn't seem to be a reason for anyone to change those patterns. Yet at the end of the first quarter of that game, I thought about the conversation he and I had about the different moments when we went against our natural tendencies—hoping for something better, something special. And when I saw him stand and cheer as one of my daughter's teammates dove for a loose ball early in the second quarter, I made a decision that some people will consider risky and even selfish.

I left my seat in the far corner of the gym and walked to where he watched the game—in the center of the stands, in the middle of the crowd. From that spot, I knew I was giving up all pretense of trying to hide from my daughter. As I sat next to him, he looked surprised. Then he flashed a smile as he wrapped his right arm around my shoulders. Yet even though he was obviously glad to have me there, and even though he always seemed to anticipate every move I made before I made it, I'm not sure that even he was prepared for what I was about to do.

As I watched the game by his side, I made <u>it my goal to view every play from his perspective</u>. Truthfully, it was one of the hardest things I've ever done. In all my years of watching my daughter play sports, I have always kept my focus on her during games: whether she was playing, how she was playing, if she was succeeding. Most parents have the same approach while watching their children play sports. It is natural and expected, and no parent can be faulted for having that approach. Still, I wanted to try his approach of focusing completely on the seemingly small and often overlooked moments of effort, selflessness and teamwork that are so important in sports. And not just focus on those moments, but celebrate them and the people who did them.

So when he stood and cheered, I stood and cheered a split second later. Sometimes, his reasons for standing and cheering were obvious, like when a player made a beautiful pass that led to a score or a player jumped into the stands to try to save a ball from going out of bounds. Other times, I had to ask him why we were standing and cheering. And he explained that a player had set a solid screen to get a teammate open or that a player had subtly helped out a teammate on defense. I also quickly learned to stand and celebrate any act of sportsmanship and respect that opponents showed each other. Once, we even saluted the interaction between a ref and a coach that started with the coach angrily questioning a call and ended with the coach and ref joking with each other.

As the game progressed, I anticipated many of the times he would stand and cheer, so we often rose in unison. By the end of the game, I also knew we had stood and cheered five times for my daughter. (Okay, so I still needed to get away from keeping statistics about her.) After the first time we clapped for her, she turned in our direction and smiled for a moment, until she saw that I was one of the two people doing it. Then her smile disappeared, and her focus returned to the game. She didn't look our way the other four times.

After the game, some parents stopped by to talk to me about the team's fifth straight win and to share compliments about my daughter. The mother of one of my daughter's teammates even approached me to comment on my cheering during the game.

"It was nice to see you being so positive toward the girls for a change," she said.

"Ah, thanks, I think," I said.

"Oh, I didn't mean to sound negative," she said. "It's just that you're not always that upbeat during. . ." She stopped herself, looking flustered.

With the situation becoming more awkward by the moment, I turned toward him, hoping he would step in and help. But then I saw he could barely hold back from laughing, and his eyes danced with mischief.

"It's nice of you to compliment him on his change," he told the woman with a straight face. "It's especially helpful because it shows him he's making progress in his therapy."

"What?!" I shrieked.

"Therapy?" the woman said, looking even more rattled.

He winked at her as he smiled and said, "I'm just kidding about the therapy, but that really was nice of you to compliment him. I've noticed the difference, too."

She relaxed for the first time since the conversation began.

"I think I'll go now before I say anything else," she said with a laugh.

As she walked away, I turned toward him again and said, "Therapy?"

"Yeah, you're right," he said. "It can't be therapy because I'm not charging you enough."

I shook my head and laughed.

"That mom was right," he said. "I don't know what got into you, but it was great to see—as enjoyable as watching the girls play."

"Just trying to look at the game in a different way," I said. "The way you do."

"How'd that feel?" he asked.

"It's not that easy, at least not for me," I said.

"Harder than your first waltz lesson?" he asked.

I laughed again. "*Nothing* could be harder than *that*."

A Small Victory

After that game, I stopped by the grocery store to pick up milk, bread and some other items that my wife said we needed. By the time I got home, my daughter was already in her room studying.

"She just went upstairs," my wife said as we put away the groceries. "It sounds like they played another great game. She was excited about that."

"She should be," I said. "Her team's playing terrific. So is she."

"Did you get a chance to tell her that?" my wife asked.

"She didn't look for me after the game," I said as I leaned against the kitchen counter. "Maybe she's being superstitious, not wanting to change her routine while the team is on a roll. Or maybe she still hasn't forgiven me yet. I really don't know. Besides, until tonight I was trying to go unnoticed at her games, since you told me that she didn't want me coming to them anymore."

"She knew you were there tonight," she said. "She talked about you when she got home."

"What did she say?" I asked.

"She said some of the girls on the team loved the way you and your friend were cheering for them."

"Good," I said. "Did she say anything about what she thought about it?"

"No," my wife said.

"Oh, okay," I said disappointedly.

"I think she's just a little cautious about you right now," she said.

"Afraid I might say or do something wrong again, huh?"

"I don't know," she said. "But I'd take it as a small victory that she told me about her teammates' reactions to you."

"Right now," I said, "I'll take any victory I can get."

A Choice to Make

He didn't waste any time writing his next note to my daughter and her teammates. She brought it home the following day, once again leaving it next to her gym bag that she dumped outside her bedroom door. I was surprised that this note began with a passing reference to me. I was even more stunned by the choices that were made by the two athletes who were featured in the note.

"Before last night's game—and congratulations, girls, on your great effort and tremendous teamwork—a friend and I were talking about some moments in life and sports. One of the thoughts that stood out from our conversation was this belief: 'Sometimes, you have to go against the usual, expected way of doing things—because you know it's the right thing to do.' So today, I'd like to share with you the stories of two athletes who made extraordinary choices.

"I heard the first story from Jack Roberts, who was the executive director of the Michigan High School Athletic Association at the time. He was giving a speech about sportsmanship, and he shared a few stories to make a point. One of his stories opened in the closing moments of a high school soccer game. A team had just scored to take a 3-2 lead with less than a minute left. The other team's senior captain took a pass, weaved past a few defenders and found himself in the clear, just needing to beat the goalie for the tying score. The captain faked one way, the goalkeeper bit, and the captain rocketed the ball into the opposite corner of the net. His teammates raced toward him in celebration, but the captain rushed toward the referee.

"Here's how Roberts described what happened next: 'The senior had noticed that the clock at the end of the field, behind the goal he had been shooting at, had ticked down to zero before he shot. He asked the referee if the scoreboard clock was official or if the referee was keeping official time on the field. The referee said the scoreboard clock was official. The senior then told the referee the kick was late, the goal shouldn't count, and the other team should win—which is what happened. It was the right thing to do, but it was also the rare thing. It made it special, very special.'

"So is what happened in the second story I want to share with you today. It involves a 7-year-old boy named Tim. He was running in a track meet where some of the events were for children in the 10-and-under division. Tim desperately wanted to win a medal in his last race of the day—the 800-meter run. As he stepped to the starting line, Tim noticed there were only four other runners in the race. He figured he had a good chance of winning one of the medals that were to be awarded to the top three finishers.

"Tim focused on that goal as he ran around the first and second turns of the 400-meter track. He still felt positive as he raced along the straightaway and headed into the third turn of the first lap. Yet between the third and fourth turns, something happened that forced Tim to make a tough choice. Another runner—a 5-year-old boy—stopped suddenly and started to cry. Seeing the boy, Tim wasn't sure whether he should continue running and pursue the medal or stop and help the other boy. Tim decided to stop. He took the 5-year-old's hand and held it, and the two boys walked together along the track until the younger boy's father met them. Tim continued the race, finishing a distant and disappointing—for him—fourth. But when he was asked about his choice later, Tim didn't regret what he did. He said, 'I just thought it was good to do that.'

"Now it's your turn. What would you have done in each situation?

"After you think about that, consider this: Sports do more than test your preparation, ability and teamwork. They also provide moments that test your integrity, your fairness and sometimes even your compassion. The choices you make in those moments define you. What do you want your choices to say about you?"

Stand and Celebrate

One streak continued, and another started at the next game. For the sixth time in a row, the girls won—with the added bonus that everyone played and contributed. One of the highlights came when a girl who rarely played hit a three-point shot late in the fourth quarter. Her teammates on the bench jumped from their seats, shouted her name and waved their white towels above their heads. With every player on the team smiling, all the moms and dads naturally enjoyed themselves, too. Some of us parents also provided our own memorable scene.

During the game, I sat with him in the middle of the stands, trying to once again match the times he cheered. It was easier this time, and he smiled and winked at me when I rose and cheered once before he did. Yet even that moment didn't compare to the highlight involving some of the other parents. It started with the mom who approached me and him after the last game, the one who told me it was nice to see me being positive toward the girls for a change. She and her husband moved to the seats right behind us early in the third quarter. I didn't notice them at first because I was so focused on everything happening on the court. But we soon became aware of her when we stood and cheered for one selfless play, and she stood and cheered a second later. We turned around, saw her and smiled at her. She smiled back at us and said, "I hope you don't mind us sitting behind you. The two of you have been cheering for the girls more than anyone else. You look like you're having so much fun that I wanted to join you."

"We're glad you're here," he said.

A few minutes later, we stood and cheered for another play, and she again stood and cheered after a slight delay. When the same situation happened a third time, she leaned her head between us and said, "This will sound stupid, but we didn't score any of the three times we stood and cheered. What have we been cheering for?"

It would have been easy to laugh, but he took the time to explain it to her—and some of the other reasons that led us to cheer.

Her face burst into a smile. "That's fantastic!" she said.

Out of the corner of my eye, I saw her husband lower his head and cover his face with his hands. Still, when we stood and cheered again, and she stood and cheered again, her husband rose and cheered with her. She was so thrilled that she gave each of us a high-five. By late in the third quarter, the four of us must have looked like we were having such a good time that six other parents joined our little block. The scene showed one of the truths about being a parent: Nothing binds parents to other parents like the shared love of their children and the shared joy of seeing them succeed.

The scene built to the moment late in the fourth quarter when the girl who rarely played hit a three-point shot. When she walked from the bench to the scorer's table two minutes earlier, the mother behind us whispered to her husband, "She's getting to play!" At first, their daughter struggled. Like many players who don't get to play too often, she was clearly nervous. She also had to overcome the natural tendency to try to do something special to prove herself. The first pass to her slipped through her hands and out of bounds. Then the person she guarded scored an easy basket. Both times, I could feel her mother cringe behind me. When my daughter smiled at the girl and motioned to her to settle down, it was the kind of moment when he and I would have normally cheered. But we both stayed seated, knowing how hard the last two plays were for the girl's parents. Still, he turned to the mom and dad and said, "She's just getting the jitters out of her system. She'll be fine. I have the feeling she's going to do something terrific."

Less than a minute later, my daughter passed her the ball as she stood behind the three-point line. The girl caught the ball, set her feet and took the shot in one smooth motion. As the ball swished through the net, her teammates erupted into a frenzy of joy for her. A similar celebration ignited among our group of parents. The girl's mother led the reaction, pounding on our shoulders as she jumped and cheered.

"Oh, I'm sorry," she said a few seconds later when she realized she was still hitting our shoulders.

"No need to apologize," he said with a smile. "We completely understand."

Her face still glowed as she whispered to us, "I'm just so happy for her."

"We all are," he said.

At the end of the game, the mom and dad who sat behind us rushed to their daughter who ran into their arms. Nearby, other parents hugged and high-fived their daughters. I looked for mine and saw her walking toward the locker room, talking and laughing with two of her coaches. At that moment, I felt a hand on my right shoulder. It was his.

"Are you okay?" he asked.

"Yeah," I said.

"I saw you looking in the direction of your daughter," he said.

"You don't miss much, do you?" I said with a smile. "I was, but I'm good. I'm happy for her. A while ago, my wife said I had to get used to her growing up and even growing away from me. Maybe I had some growing up to do, too. Right now, it's just important how she feels."

He nodded and smiled at me. "I'm proud of you," he said.

"Gee, thanks, dad," I said. Both of us laughed.

"We need to celebrate," he said. "The team. Your daughter. Your growing up."

We laughed again.

"Seriously," he said, "I've been meaning to invite you to this great Italian restaurant. Is there an evening this week that works for you?"

I tried to think of any family conflicts we might have. "Wednesday should be good," I said.

"Great," he said. "I'll meet you here at the school, and we can drive there together."

It would turn out to be the night when I asked him about his nickname, the night when he told me his thoughts about when God cheers.

It would also be the night when I understood the relationship I wanted to have with my daughter.

When God Cheers

I was waiting outside the gym entrance on Wednesday evening when he drove up in his light blue Chevy Nova. As I walked toward the car, our friend Dan headed toward the gym to pick up his son from basketball practice. Dan's face lit up with mischief when he saw the two of us together.

"You must be a real challenge if he's spending extra time with you outside of games," Dan said to me with a smile. Turning to him, Dan added, "Obviously, you have a lot of patience, 'God.'"

"I learned it from those years of working with you," he said.

The three of us laughed. When Dan continued walking toward the gym, I got in the car.

"Are you ready for some of the best Italian food you'll ever eat?" he asked as I buckled my seat belt.

"I love Italian food," I said.

"Good. Then you'll love Marie's. Great people. Great food."

As he pulled out of the school's parking lot, I said, "There's one thing that Dan mentioned that I've wanted to ask you about. What's your reaction to him calling you 'God'?"

He smiled. "There are a few things I've learned about nicknames, especially when guys give them," he said. "You probably know them, too. One is that if you're a guy, you'll get at least one nickname growing up, and probably more. And you don't have a choice about what nickname other guys will give you. Another reality is that no matter what you do in life or how many years have passed since you got that nickname, some of your old friends will still remember it and call you it. At least with this nickname, I know it's said with respect and appreciation, so I just roll with it. You can't take everything seriously. Besides, I'm not the only one who's been called that. No doubt, you've heard of Vince Lombardi, the great football coach who led the Green Bay Packers to a lot of championships. One of his players, Paul Hornung, told this story about Lombardi: 'One night, after a long, cold, difficult day, Lombardi came home late and tumbled into bed. "God," his wife said, "your feet are cold." And Lombardi answered, "Around the house, dear, you may call me Vince."'

"I love that story. You have to have a sense of humor at times. If you can't change something, accept it and make the most of it. Even have fun with it."

"You have more fun and more perspective at a game than anyone I've ever known," I said as he turned left at a light. "How did you get that way?"

"Have you ever thought about when God would cheer?" he responded.

"No," I said.

"Do you think he would cheer just for the team or the athlete that won?" he asked. "Do you think he would applaud just the game-winning home run or the 30-foot putt that dropped on the 18th hole? Would he only be thrilled seeing a swimmer earn another Olympic medal, a track star break a world record, a tennis pro win Wimbledon, or a volleyball team win a national championship? If you think about it, that approach is far too limiting for him, especially considering what he calls us to do in life. Sacrifice. Give completely. Commit yourself to others. Make the most of your talents. Reach out to your enemy. Be part of something bigger than yourself. Put everything you have on the line. The list goes on and on. And nothing on that list is easy. They're hard and demanding. And all those qualities can be part of sports. In fact, they are *the best part* of sports. *And* the best part of us. So God wouldn't cheer merely because some team wins or because someone is a gifted athlete. He would save his best cheers for something more special than those measures of success. He would cheer for any team or any athlete of any skill level when they do in sports what he asks them to do in life. And he would cheer loudly. That's why I cheer the way I do."

"Do you really think God cares about sports?" I asked. "A lot of people tell me that I put too much emphasis on sports."

"That is so hard to believe," he said with a laugh.

"Okay, okay, I deserve that," I said.

"I'm just giving you a hard time," he said. "A lot of people tell me the same thing about people putting too much emphasis on sports, and that God doesn't care about sports." He paused for a moment as he looked in the rear view mirror and then over his right shoulder to see if he was clear to get in the right lane. Once he did, he continued, "Look, it's hard to deny that people put too much emphasis on sports. But I still have no doubt that God cares about sports. He gives people the talents to play them. They bring us together, they give us joy, and sometimes they teach us about life, faith and hope. They also teach us about pain, loss and the courage it takes to get back up when we fail or fall. Besides, if *we* care about sports, and *he* cares about us, it seems only natural that he would care about sports, too—if only from the standpoint of how they influence our lives and our relationships, even our relationship with him."

He slowed down and flicked on the right turn signal.

"Here we are," he said as he pulled into the parking lot near a red-brick building that looked like it had once been a house. The name of the restaurant—Marie's—was bathed in lights.

"So let me get this straight," I said as he switched off the ignition. "You think God not only cares about sports, but he cheers, too."

"That's right," he said.

"And the next thing you'll tell me is that he likes popcorn when he cheers at a game," I said.

"Who doesn't?" he said with a smile. "So you think I'm crazy?"

"No, I'm just returning the favor of giving you a hard time," I said. "Actually, you should be more worried because what you said makes sense to me. I like the idea of 'when God cheers.'"

"Good," he said. "That's another reason to celebrate: We agree about something. Now let's eat."

Seconds later, we were out of the car and stepping onto the porch of the restaurant. He held the door open for me.

"You will love this place," he raved.

"The food is that good?" I asked.

"It's more than the food," he said. "Much more."

A Bargain with God

While the outside of the restaurant looked like a house, the inside felt like a home from the Old World or "the old neighborhood." Family photos filled the walls from the entryway to the hostess desk. Frank Sinatra crooned "Come Rain or Come Shine" on the restaurant's sound system. A peek into the main dining room revealed tables and booths topped with white tablecloths and fresh flower combinations of soft yellows and light blues. A waiter passed by carrying a tray filled with huge portions of pasta covered in a red sauce—or "gravy" as they called it here. It looked and smelled so wonderful that my head turned instinctively toward the aroma. Everything combined to create the feeling of "Welcome, we're glad you're here, stay a while, you're home."

Yet, while the atmosphere and the food at Marie's made for one of the best dining experiences I've ever had, it wasn't the real reason he brought me there. He really invited me to Marie's for a story. It was a story that was captured in the framed photo overlooking table 29, the table he had reserved for us that night.

"Do you recognize either one of the two people in that photo?" he asked shortly after the waitress took our order and brought an antipasto for us to share.

The framed black-and-white photo showed two young waiters with their arms around each other's shoulders, smiling. As I scanned their faces, I was struck by something familiar about the guy on the right. There was something about the combination of his nose, hair and chin, but I still couldn't place him.

"Think of a famous singer at a much younger age," he hinted. When I still didn't recognize the guy, he added, "He left his heart in San Francisco."

"Tony Bennett," I said. "Oh yeah, now I see it."

"He was a singing waiter during high school in New York," he said. "He took the job to help his mother take care of the family during the Great Depression. His father died when he was nine. He later said that his time as a singing waiter made him realize he wanted to make a living by singing." He smiled and added, "It seems to have worked out okay for him."

I smiled and nodded. Then I asked, "Should I know the other guy in the picture?"

"No," he said, "but I'm glad you asked about him. His name was Sal. He had a great voice, too. He was a few years older than Tony. Sal got married right after high school and moved to New York with his wife, Gina. He wanted to become a big time singer. And he took a job as a singing waiter to help pay the bills. By their second anniversary, Gina was pregnant. But it was a tough pregnancy, and there was a period of time when it looked like the baby wouldn't make it. Sal prayed a lot during that time. He even reached the point where he bargained with God, saying he'd give up his dream of a singing career if God would let the child live. The doctors weren't sure how it happened, but Gina gave birth to a healthy girl. Sal and Gina named her Marie, as a tribute to the Blessed Mother. A short while later, the new family left New York and moved back home. Sal got a job as a waiter, learned the business of running a restaurant, and eventually opened his own. This is the place—Marie's."

I smiled. "And I thought you brought me here for the food," I said. "You just had another story for me."

He grinned. "There's *always* a story," he said.

"I'm beginning to see that," I said. "But let me ask you one question about Sal's story."

"What's that?" he asked.

"Do you think God wanted Sal to keep that bargain? Giving up his dream of a singing career?"

"It's a good question," he said. "From my viewpoint, God doesn't require people to keep those kinds of bargains. He doesn't want us to give up our dreams or stop using our talents. But I also believe those bargains make us think about what's important and essential in our lives. I also have the benefit of hearing what Sal said later about that bargain. He told me that when Marie's life was in the balance, it crystallized for him what mattered most to him. And that was his wife and child. Here's another thing you should know about Sal. He kept singing through the years. Right here in this restaurant."

He pointed to a piano in a corner.

"Sal would play the piano," he continued. "He'd sing a few songs every night and do a small show every Wednesday. It brought in the people on a usually slow night for business. He especially liked doing the hits of Tony Bennett. He'd tell people the story of how he once was a singing waiter with Tony. He'd wink and say that he taught Tony everything he knew."

"Is Sal still alive?" I asked.

"No, he died five years ago," he said. "He was a good man. Had a good life. He always said he had the love of his wife and his daughter, and he couldn't ask for more than that."

"What about Marie?" I asked.

"There's a story there, too," he said.

"Of course," I said with a smile.

"She was also blessed with a great voice," he said. "She went to New York for a while. She never made it big, but she did some cabaret work and had a fair share of small singing roles in shows. Sal and Gina went to see her perform as much as they could. Sal would come back from those trips, and he couldn't stop smiling. After about ten years in New York, Marie moved back here. She and her husband had two small children by then, and she wanted them to be closer to her parents. From time to time, she'd come into the restaurant on Wednesday nights and sing with her dad. Then she started helping at the restaurant and eventually began running it as her parents got older." He nodded toward a woman who had just approached a couple at a table across the room. The woman smiled and talked with them. "That's Marie," he said.

When she turned to our side of the room moments later, she flashed a look that seemed to suggest that she recognized him. Then she was sure. She smiled as she stopped at our table and softly said, "You're my dad's angel. The one with the terrific voice."

I wanted to ask her what she meant by calling him "my dad's angel," but she was focused on him.

"It's nice to see you again, Marie," he said, returning her smile. He motioned toward me and added, "I'd like you to meet a friend of mine. It's his first time here. I told him you have the best Italian food ever."

"You're absolutely right," she said, making all three of us laugh.

Based upon what he had told me about the time frame of her birth, I figured she had to be in her 60s, but she looked about 20 years younger. Her face showed no wrinkles. Her shoulder-length, dark brown hair betrayed no hints of gray. Her brown eyes radiated warmth and light. She looked trim and stylish in black dress pants and a black sequined top.

"It's strange," she said, looking at him. "I was thinking about you earlier this week. Monday was the fifth anniversary of my dad dying. I think his funeral was the last time I saw you."

"It was," he said. Then he stood, put his hands on top of the chair next to his and asked, "Do you have some time to sit with us?"

"Sure," she said, sitting next to him. "I don't begin singing for another ten minutes."

"I was telling my friend about your dad and Tony Bennett," he said. "And the way that you and your dad sang here every Wednesday."

She looked at me, motioned toward him and asked, "Did he also tell you about the time that he sang with my dad?"

I smiled and shook my head, "No, he left out that story."

"It doesn't surprise me," she said, turning to him and smiling warmly. "It was ten years ago. One of the Tony Bennett songs that my dad sang every Wednesday was a love song called 'Because of You.' My dad would have one of the waiters or waitresses go into the kitchen where my mom was cooking and have her come into the dining room. She always protested that she was too busy, but she always came eventually. And when he saw her, he would sing 'Because of You' to her. And every week, the song ended the same—with my mom sitting next to my dad at the piano, both of them singing the last couple of lines together, and them hugging each other."

"It was a beautiful thing to see," he said.

Marie touched his left hand and continued. "Well, two weeks after my mom died, my dad sat down at the piano to sing for the first time since she died. And halfway through his list of songs, he began to sing 'Because of You.' As a tribute to my mom. But he couldn't finish the song. It broke my heart. I wanted to help him, but I couldn't move. I was crying, too. And just then, your friend here gets up from this very table, sits next to my dad at the piano, puts his arm around him and starts singing the song. My dad was so shocked that he began singing again. And they finished the song together. It was beautiful, and there wasn't a dry eye in the place."

She nodded at him and said, "That's why I call him 'my dad's angel with the terrific voice.' My dad said later that he thought he was singing with Tony Bennett himself."

As he smiled and lowered his head, she looked across the table at me and asked, "Did he tell you about the bargain my dad made with God?"

"Yes," I said.

She looked at the framed photo of her dad and Tony Bennett as young men, and it was like the years melted away for her.

"He always told me that he got the better part of that bargain with God," she said softly. "But I was the one who was blessed. When I needed someone to cheer for me, he was there. When I needed someone to comfort me, he was there. He could be tough when I needed that, too. There wasn't one day when I doubted that I could count on him or that he loved me. That's all a child can ask for. That's all a child really wants. He was a wonderful husband and a terrific father."

When our waitress served our meals seconds later, Marie excused herself, saying it was time for her to sing. As amazing as the food was, it was hard to focus on eating while she sang. Her voice was just that good, that soulful. "Because of You" was the last song on her playlist. Before she sang it, she told the story of how her father always dedicated the song to her mother every Wednesday night. Then she dedicated the song to both of them. Midway through the lyrics, she looked across the room to where we were sitting and winked at him. He subtly raised his glass of wine toward her and nodded.

When we left Marie's later, I told him, "You were right."

"About what?" he asked as we walked toward his car.

"You told me I would love this place, but not just for the food. 'For much more,' you said."

"Anything stand out the most to you?" he asked.

"What Marie said about her dad, about the way he was as a father," I said. "I hope my daughter can come even close to thinking of me in that way some day. I want to be that kind of father."

"Hmmm," he said.

"Why did you say that?" I asked.

"When I asked you what stood out the most to you about tonight, I figured you would say the part where Marie's father thought I sang just like Tony Bennett."

We both laughed.

"All kidding aside, you do have an amazing voice," I told him as we stood by his car. "But that isn't what stands out about you anymore. At least not to me. It's the way you connect with people, the way you bring out the best in them. Like with Marie and Sal. You have a gift in that way."

"Thanks," he said. "But I don't consider it a gift. I see it as a privilege. These people let me get to know them. They share their stories with me. I'm the one who's blessed."

He moved to the driver's side of the car and opened the door. Leaning against the car, he winked at me and said, "Of course, the flip side is that I sometimes meet people who tell me to get the hell away from them the first time we meet." He stood there, grinning at me.

"I can't believe you just said that," I said in mock disgust. "I just gave you a compliment, and you come back with that?! I'm hurt. I'm truly hurt."

He just laughed. So did I. As we got into the car, I put on my seat belt and told him, "You *wish* you had a voice like Tony Bennett."

His laughter filled the car as we left Marie's.

An Unexpected Discovery

When I got home that night, the stories of Marie and Sal still filled my mind. I headed toward my daughter's bedroom, hoping she was awake, wanting to just say "Good night" to her. But there was no light showing from beneath her bedroom door. Still, I opened the door and peeked toward her bed. She was asleep. Standing by the door, I made the sign of the cross toward her and whispered, "I love you." Heading downstairs, I made my usual nightly round of turning off the lights and making sure the doors were locked. Walking through the living room, I saw her backpack by a chair, with an opened envelope on top of the backpack. Another story from him, I figured. I could feel my anticipation rising as I walked toward the envelope. Yet, when I picked up the envelope with his handwriting on the front, it was empty inside. I looked around the backpack and under it, but there wasn't a note to be found.

A Salute to a Friend

I arrived earlier than usual for the next game. I wanted to savor every second of a season that had become more special with each passing week, a season in which there were only three games left on the schedule. Having extra time, I stopped by the concession stand where a couple of volunteers began to grill hot dogs while the first batch of popcorn popped in the machine.

"What can I get you?" one of the volunteers asked me.

"Two popcorns," I said, handing her a five dollar bill.

"It's almost ready," she said, taking my money and giving me back three ones. "The girls are really having a great season."

"Thanks," I said. "It's been a lot of fun."

She turned and saw that the popcorn was ready. Seconds later, she handed me two bags and said, "Enjoy the popcorn and the game."

I nodded, smiled and turned toward the gym. Inside, I searched to see if he was already there, but he wasn't. I headed toward our usual place in the middle of the stands, leaned one bag of popcorn against the bleacher by my feet and started munching on my popcorn. Soon, the other parents began to arrive, taking seats near me. We smiled and high-fived each other while exchanging compliments about our daughters and comments about the upcoming game. With the team's extended stretch of success, our parent group had become tight, close. I even got a hug from the mom who once told me, "It was nice to see you being so positive toward the girls for a change." After the hug, she said, "This is so exciting! Jenny told us that if the girls win one of their last three games they'll play in the championship!"

I hadn't known that until just then. It made me think of the possibilities of winning a championship. It also made me tense in a way I hadn't felt since early in the season.

"By the way," she said, "where's your friend?"

"He should be here soon," I said. "I've got some popcorn waiting for him."

He wasn't there when our group of parents stood together and cheered our girls as they ran onto the court for warm-ups. He still wasn't there just before the game started and I kept looking at the gym doors, waiting for him to appear, waiting for his smile, waiting for him to lead us in cheers. In fact, he wasn't there for any part of the game, a game in which the team played its worst basketball in a long time.

The game began promisingly with the girls taking a 10-2 lead. The teammates on the court smiled at each other. The players on the bench encouraged the girls on the floor. And our group of parents rose and cheered for each unselfish play and each display of extra effort. Then nearly everything fell apart. Sloppy passes resulted in steals and easy baskets for the other team, which led their players to grow in confidence as they took and made other shots, which led to our girls getting discouraged on defense and pressing on offense. The only bright spot for our team—and I say this as objectively as a parent can—was my daughter. She made most of her shots, she kept encouraging her teammates, and she tried to will her team to a win. When the other coach had his players double-team her, she passed the ball to her teammates for open shots. But it was just one of those games when the shots of the other players didn't fall.

A similar scene unfolded in the stands. As my daughter's teammates struggled, their parents found it harder and harder to stand and cheer whenever someone on our team showed extra effort or unselfishness. During an extended stretch in the second half, I stood alone at times, still trying to praise those plays. But I have to admit it was a struggle. The only thing that kept me standing and cheering was recalling how he had stood alone and cheered during those early games of the season. With just a few minutes left in this one, my daughter made a steal while helping out a teammate. As I rose and clapped—alone again—I realized that some other parents may have thought I was focused solely on my daughter. And she did glance up at me when I did it. But it wasn't just a cheer for her, it was also a salute to him.

In the end, the girls lost by 12 points to a team with a losing record.

As she left the bleachers with her husband, the mom who hugged me before the game said, "We missed your friend today."

I missed him, too.

Missing a Shot

I had to work late the next night. When I got home, my wife made a ham-and-turkey sandwich for me, and we talked about our days. When I asked about our daughter, my wife told me she was up in her room studying for two tests.

"She asked about you, too," my wife said. "At dinner, she wanted to know when you were coming home."

"That's nice to hear," I said. "I didn't think she thought too much about me lately."

"She's a busy girl these days," my wife said. "Sometimes, I'm not sure how kids today have time for everything and everyone in their lives. It's overwhelming."

"You're right," I said. "I just miss her smile and her laugh. And just talking to her."

"That reminds me," my wife said. "Before dinner, she was in the living room, and I heard her laughing and then crying. I went in and asked her if she was okay. She said she was fine, that she was just reading a note she got from a friend at school today. She wouldn't say anymore about it."

"I wonder what it was about," I said. "It would have been nice to hear her laugh."

After I finished the sandwich, I went into the living room and saw my daughter's backpack near a chair again, with another opened envelope on top of it. Reaching for the envelope, I found that this one was empty, too. I slumped in the chair and flipped on a basketball game on the television, figuring that my daughter would need something from her backpack after a while. When she did, I could at least say hello and ask about her day. But the next thing I knew, two hours had passed and my wife was waking me, telling me it was time for bed. I noticed that my daughter's backpack was already zipped and ready for her to take to school the next day. The envelope was gone, too. She had been there, and I had missed her. I slumped up the stairs to bed.

A Game to Remember

I didn't see him [God] at the next game either. And if there was a game during that season when I needed him to be with me the most, it was that one. As it happens in many games, there are numerous plays that influence the outcome, but the focus often falls on a select few. In this case, the spotlight shined on one play, and it involved my daughter.

Until the last few seconds, this game was one my daughter would like to forget, based upon the way she thinks she played overall. And yet it's a game both of us will always remember.

Unlike the previous game, my daughter struggled with her shooting in this one. She connected on just one of her first eight shots. Still, she played hard and unselfishly. So did her teammates. Fortunately, her teammates also made enough baskets to keep the game close. Their team trailed by one point with ten seconds left when their coach called for a timeout. As I watched the team huddle around Coach Miller, I remembered one of the things that he stressed during a meeting with parents and players before the season started. He said, "In practice, we will focus on improving the areas where we need to get better and preparing for the games ahead. But in games, I don't want the girls worrying about any mistakes they make or shots they miss. Our focus will always be on doing our best in *this* play, *this* moment." It's a great approach to have. In basketball. In life. It's also one of the hardest things to embrace, no matter what your age, no matter what the situation. Yet as my daughter walked from the huddle, she had a confident look.

After the game, I learned that my daughter wasn't the first option to take the shot on the play. But when the ball was passed to her with five seconds left and everyone else was tightly guarded, she didn't hesitate. She faked a shot and drove past her defender as the clock ticked to four seconds. She raced into the lane with three seconds left. She released the shot with just one second left, right before she collided with a player from the other team who tried to cut off her path to the basket. As a ref's whistle sounded, all the eyes in the gym focused on the ball rising to the rim. The ball caught the inside right edge of the rim and spun around the whole rim one time and then another. With everyone in the gym leaning forward, the ball finally dropped into the net, setting off an explosion of joy among my daughter's team, Coach Miller and our fans. In that moment, I felt such happiness for my daughter and pride in her. Only the formality of her taking a free throw—because the ref had whistled a foul on her shot—was left before the girls could celebrate making it to the championship game. Only the foul shot remained before I could head down to the court to hug my daughter and tell her how terrific she was, how proud of her I was. It was the storybook moment I had imagined in all those years of helping her practice in the back yard.

But it didn't happen that way. During the suspense and celebration of her shot falling through the net, I and nearly everyone in the gym thought the ref had whistled a foul on the girl who cut off my daughter's path to the basket. Instead, as my daughter and her teammates continued to jump into each other's arms, the ref signaled that it was an offensive foul on my daughter and the basket didn't count. In a flash, celebration turned to confusion, and joy changed to heartbreak for our side of the gym. As the ref explained her call to an incredulous yet classy Coach Miller, our girls looked shocked, like something special had been taken away from them in a flash. A couple of our parents shouted at the ref. Then came the moment that my daughter and I will never forget—because it was just so unexpected for both of us. In the midst of the confusion, the anger and the heartbreak, a voice from the stands called out my daughter's name and yelled, "Gutsy play. Great try."

Caught up in all the emotions of that moment, I almost turned around and looked for him when I heard those words. But it wasn't him who said them. It was me. I walked down from the stands, into the chaos on the court and toward the ref who made the call. I rushed past the ref and toward my daughter, wrapping her in my arms. And here's the best part: She hugged me back.

Learning from a Loss, Revealing a Joyful Mystery

There comes a time in nearly every sports book or movie when everything builds to a climax—a dramatic moment when a team that has fought against the odds achieves redemption, validation or definition in a championship setting. Yet the reality is that most teams and athletes don't make it to a championship moment. And most teams and athletes end their seasons with a loss.

Like many people, I've always viewed success in sports by the golden glow of a championship trophy, by the unbridled joy of the winners. It's hard to escape that view in a culture that constantly shines the spotlight on the winners and quickly sweeps the losing team or losing athlete to the curb. That perspective has played out in my family's home for most of the seasons my daughter has played sports. After a win, an air of light and life filled the house. After a loss, silence and a sense of heaviness marked our home.

I thought about that perspective as I drove home that night. I thought about how the girls had played hard together and believed in each other the entire game. I thought about how, with tears in their eyes and stunned looks on their faces, they lined up to shake the hands of the players on the other team. I thought about how Coach Miller kept his calm and his class. I thought about how my daughter still believed in herself and took the risk of taking the last shot. I also thought about him. I thought about what he had said to me when he sat down behind me in that game early in the season: "She needs you to believe in her." As all those thoughts ran through my mind, I realized for the first time what people with a better perspective and more balance to their lives have long known: Even in a loss—and maybe especially in a loss—people could redeem, validate and define themselves.

I was still considering that reality in our living room when my daughter came home that night. After she put her gym bag down, she reached into it and pulled three envelopes from it. She crossed the room to where I sat on the couch and sat next to me.

"You should know about these," she said, holding the envelopes out to me.

I recognized his handwriting on the front of the envelopes, but I pretended I didn't know what they were or who wrote them.

"What are those?" I asked.

She smiled. "He said you would act like you didn't know about them." She shook her head and laughed. I can't tell you what a joy it was to hear her laugh again.

"He told me about how he had shared with you that Coach Miller asked him to write notes about team values to us girls."

"Oh, so those are some of the notes?" I asked.

"Seriously, Dad?" she said with a smile. "He said you were probably reading every note he sent to me."

Learning from a Loss, Revealing a Joyful Mystery

"Okay, so I did," I confessed. "They were near your gym bag, and the envelopes were open. I like the stories he tells. And besides, it was a way to feel connected to you, too. To read something you were reading."

She nodded and looked touched by what I had said.

"That's why he told me to make sure you didn't see his last three notes to me, unless I wanted you to see them or until I was ready to show them to you," she said. "That's why two of these envelopes were empty when they were by my backpack in the past few days. And I just found the last one in my basketball locker after school today."

"Are they different from the other ones he wrote?" I asked.

"Yes," she said, handing me the three envelopes. "These three letters were just for me. They're all about you and me."

The first note shared the story of the beach vacation when I closed my eyes in the Jacuzzi while she sat on the edge of it.

"I had never heard that story before," she said. "It sent a shiver down my spine."

"I'm sorry," I said.

"For what?"

"For closing my eyes. For almost..."

"You found me," she said. "You lifted me up."

"I thought I had lost you."

"I know," she said. "It helps explain why you sometimes go overboard in trying to protect me."

The second note told the story of how I took dance lessons to learn how to waltz with her.

"That one made me laugh and cry," she said.

"Was that the one you were reading when Mom asked you about it?" I said.

"Yeah," she said.

"We did a nice job that night," I said.

"Yeah," she said with a smile. "We did."

The third story was written in my own words, the story of the evening of the baseball game when we caught that home run ball together.

"My favorite part of that story was reading how I helped you believe in hope and magic again," she said. "I didn't know I could do that for you."

"You do. For Mom, too," I said. "It's one of the reasons we love you so much."

"Thanks, Dad," she said. "And thanks for tonight at the game. It really made a difference to know you were there for me—even when I played so bad and messed up at the end."

"You didn't..." I tried to protest, but she cut me off.

"It doesn't matter," she said. "That game's over. We still have another. But seeing you stand up for me...that meant a lot. So do these stories."

I savored that feeling and that moment as long as I could. Beyond anything else I had learned during this season, I now understood that whatever time I had with my daughter was precious—and slipping away more with each year. I just wanted to enjoy the time I had with her, the time I had of being her father.

She rested her head on my shoulder for a few minutes. Neither of us talked during that time. After a while, she was on her feet again, saying she had to study for a Spanish test. She hugged me again and headed toward the stairs. As I watched her walk away, I thanked God for her. I also thanked God for "God." With his work on me and his stories to my daughter, he had saved me from what would have been one of the greatest losses of my life.

I just wondered where he had been the last two games. I even began to fear that I might never see him again.

Making a Comeback

It was the last game of the regular season, the last opportunity for the girls to play for the championship. I arrived early again and looked for him in the gym. He wasn't there so I headed toward the concession stand, hoping he was talking with the volunteers and complimenting them on the popcorn. "It's the best I've ever tasted, and I've tasted a lot," he always told them. But he wasn't there either. My friend Dan was, making sure the volunteers had all the supplies they needed.

"Hey," he greeted me. "Big game tonight. That was a tough one the other night. I couldn't believe that call the ref made at the end of the game, but 'God' said. . ."

"What?" I said, cutting in on him. "You guys were at the last game? Where? I was looking for him the whole game."

"He asked me if he could watch the game from the storage room that's in a corner of the gym," Dan said. "I asked him why, and he said he just wanted a place where he could watch the game without anyone seeing him. The storage room has two doors with windows on each of them. He liked that he could see the court and the home bleachers from there. I told him it was fine with me. He watched the last two games from there."

"Two games?" I asked.

"Yeah," Dan said. "I didn't watch the first game with him, but I went in there for the last part of the second game, just to see how he was doing. As you know, it's interesting watching a game with him. He really enjoys watching our girls play. He was also complimenting some of the things the other team did, too. The big difference was that he didn't clap and cheer like he does when he's in the stands. And when Coach Miller called timeout at the end of the game, he did something I didn't understand."

"What was that?" I asked.

"When the girls went back on the court, he left the storage room and stood at the edge of the visitors' bleachers," Dan said. "I followed him and said, 'I thought you didn't want anyone to see you?' He said he has learned that when people get so focused on something you can be right there among them, and many times they don't even pay attention to you. He also reminded me of what he had once told me when we were refs together—how the endings of close games often produce the most memorable moments. And he wanted to see this one up close.

"He was right about everything. Everyone's focus was on the court and those next few seconds. And when your daughter drove into the lane and made the shot, and everyone celebrated, it was just one of those special moments. Then the ref called the foul on her. I told him, 'The ref got that one wrong.' He just said, 'Tough call.' He said it very calmly. That's when I looked at him. He was watching the court, taking in everything. He looked up at one point, and his eyes narrowed. He started smiling and nodding. And then it seemed like there were tears in his eyes. I tried to see what he was looking at, but there was so much going on. I asked him if he was okay. He just patted me on the shoulder, said, 'Thanks, Dan,' and walked out of the gym."

Dan paused, laughed and said, "He's different from anyone I've ever met. He's a mysterious guy in a lot of ways. Sometimes, he's right there with you. Other times, he seems to disappear from your life. But once you get to know him, he has this impact that stays with you."

"I know the feeling," I said. "Is he coming to tonight's game?"

"He didn't say," Dan said. He looked at his watch and excused himself. "Hey, I've got to run," he said. "I've got to get some more drinks and hot dogs for the concession stand. Good luck to the girls tonight."

As Dan walked away, I turned and ordered two bags of popcorn.

When I entered the gym, I looked for the storage room and found it. Then I scanned the stands. He was there, in his usual spot, in the middle of our parent group. Moms were hugging him, and the dads were high-fiving him as I climbed the bleachers. Waiting until the hugs and high-fives ended, I raised a bag of popcorn toward him. He nodded and smiled.

"What's with all the hugs and high-fives?" I asked.

"They said they missed me," he said. "That was nice of them."

"So I guess you didn't tell them you were watching the last two games from that storage room over there," I said as I sat beside him.

He smiled and said, "I wondered how long it would take Dan to tell you about that."

"By the way, you owe me two dollars for the popcorn," I said.

"Two dollars? It was just a buck a bag last week."

"This bag is free," I said. "You owe me for the two bags I bought you the past two games. If I'd known you were in the storage room,

I'd have delivered them to you. Seriously, why did you want to watch the game alone from there?"

"Sometimes it's good to see things from a different perspective," he said. "The time seemed right for me to step out of the center of everything."

"What was it like watching from there?" I asked.

"I could see everything," he said. "But they keep the wrestling mats in there. I've been in places that smell better."

"You should have told me where you were," I said. "I really could have used you by my side the past two games, especially during the ending of the last one."

"But we both would have missed the best moment of the season," he said. "That hug between you and your daughter. . .that was a moment to remember forever."

As I turned to look at him, everything started to sink in for me. He didn't want to watch the game from the storage room for himself. It was to let me be in the stands without him, without the benefit of following his lead. And it struck me that if he hadn't given me that freedom, it's doubtful I would have stood on my own at the end of that game and cheered for my daughter. And it's doubtful it would have meant that much to her if he was beside me, doing the same thing. I realized he had stepped aside those two games to give me the opportunity to step up on my own. And he wasn't just rooting for the girls from his secret spot, he was rooting for me. He had been rooting for me all season.

I was tempted to ask him if all my connections were right, but I didn't. I *knew* I was right. Instead, I told him about everything that happened at our house after that game. He smiled and nodded as I shared the details. And he was clearly touched when I mentioned the part about my daughter resting her head on my shoulder. Still, I gave him a hard time about instructing my daughter to not leave the three stories in their envelopes.

"I can't believe you told her to keep them away from me, that I had been reading your notes to the team all along," I said in mock disbelief.

"Hey, I *know* you," he said. We both laughed.

Those good feelings continued on the court. Any worries of a heartbreak hangover from the last game disappeared quickly as the girls shot out to a lead. And the lead kept growing, thrilling our fans who found numerous opportunities to cheer for the girls' hustle, teamwork and unselfishness. We savored every second of it. When the game ended, the girls danced and hugged. Some of them shouted, "We're in the championship!" In the midst of the joyous scene, my daughter bounded up the bleachers, getting high-fives and congratulations from every parent she passed. When she reached the two of us, she hugged us both.

"Congratulations," he told her. "I love the way your team bounced back from early in the season and after the last game. You should be proud of yourselves."

"Thank you," she told him. "And thanks for all the notes."

Soon, she bounded down the bleachers, joining a dance with her teammates.

"She's one of my favorites," he said as we watched the girls celebrate.

"Thanks for bringing her back to me," I said. "I was telling my wife this morning about everything that happened last night between me and our daughter. And how special it was. I also told her that you weren't there for the game again, and how I missed that. It got me thinking back to when you invited me to Lenny's for a Reuben. Before we ate, you gave thanks for the food. Then you gave thanks for me joining you for lunch—and what you hoped would be the blessing of a new friend. You may find this hard to believe, but I was hoping for the same thing. And here we are. So thanks."

"Thanks to you, too," he said.

I thought about making a joke at that point, or saying, "Yeah, but you still owe me two bucks for the popcorn." Something to lighten up the moment. But I didn't, and neither did he. It just seemed right for once to let the worth of our friendship be shared aloud and celebrated—in a season filled with reasons for celebration.

The Best Compliment in Sports

He gave his last note to the girls on the day before the championship game. He also gave an extra one to my daughter to take home to me. The note included many of the thoughts he had shared with me about the way he believes God cheers.

"Thank you for the joy I've had in watching your team play this season," he began. "I know that everyone of you will do everything you can to win the championship, and I hope you play the best game of your season. Yet right now, I want to compliment you on what has already made you special. If you've noticed me in the stands during games, you've probably figured out that I don't stand and cheer when you make a shot. I stand and cheer for other reasons.

"In fact, a friend once asked me why I cheer the way I do. I told him that I try to cheer the way that I imagine God would. In my mind, God wouldn't cheer merely because some team wins or because someone is a gifted athlete. He would save his best cheers

123

for something more special than those measures of success. He would cheer for any athlete of any skill level when they do in sports what he asks them to do in life. Sacrifice. Give completely. Commit yourselves to others. Make the most of your talents. Reach out to your opponent. Be part of something bigger than yourselves. Put everything you have on the line.

"You have showed all those qualities as a team. You have showed them after a tough stretch in your season and after a heartbreaking loss. One of my favorite motivational slogans in sports is, 'Play like a champion.' It's an approach to sports that has endured for decades. It's an approach to sports that doesn't measure you as a champion by whether you win. It measures you by the way you play. And I love the way your team plays. I believe you are a team that God would cheer. I can't think of a better compliment to give you."

Playing Like a Champion

I began the story of this magical season by making a confession. Now, I need to make an apology. Or at least offer an explanation.

For a story about a magical season that leads to a championship, people naturally expect to learn about the outcome of the game, with all the dramatic details included. The championship involving my daughter's team kept everyone on the edge of their seats that night. And there's no doubt that the tense, intense game led more than a few people to pray, beg and bargain with God to let their team win.

As for me, I also made a bargain with him.

When I told him I was thinking about writing a story about this season, he was thrilled—especially when I told him it would focus on the bond of a parent and a child, how we lose each other sometimes, and how we hopefully find our way back to each other.

"A story!" he said. "Maybe I've rubbed off on you after all! I can't wait to see how you put it all together."

"Would it be okay with you if I also included the part about you and me, and the stories you shared with the girls?" I asked.

He hesitated. "That would be fine," he finally said. "There's just one thing I would like you to do for me in return, if you would consider it. There may be parts of the story that I want you to change. If, after reading your version, I want to change one part, would you do it?"

Without hesitation, I said, "Sure." After all he had done for me, it was the least I could do.

I just was surprised when he told me that he wanted me to change the part about the championship game.

"I thought I did a good job of capturing the drama and the emotions of the game," I said, more defensively than I wanted to sound.

"You did," he said. "It's terrific."

"Then why do you want me to change it?" I asked.

"I think it would be better if the emphasis was different," he said.

"I'm not sure I know what you mean," I said.

"The emphasis is on the score," he said.

"I don't emphasize the score," I said.

"It doesn't matter," he said. "As soon as you mention the score, as soon as you say who won and who lost, it changes everything. The score always has a way of defining a game, of affecting people's perceptions and eclipsing everything that matters—especially in a championship."

"But you can't tell about the championship without mentioning the score!" I said.

"You could," he said.

I shook my head back and forth. I was incredulous.

"But people will want to know the score," I said. "They'll want to know if they should feel happy for the girls or sad for them."

"They just need to be proud of them, for putting their efforts and their hearts on the line," he said. He sighed, "Look, we could debate this forever. I know most people want to know the score, and I know some people will feel cheated that they don't know whether the girls won or lost. But this time, let's keep the score out of the equation for people. Let's keep the focus on what matters more. That's the change I want you to make, please. Will you do it?"

I relented.

Still, I realize that many people will try to draw their own conclusions about the outcome of the game. Some will infer that my description of the season as "magical" and my lobbying for the score to be mentioned mean the girls won the championship. Others will infer that his insistence that the score not be included is a sign that the girls lost, and he didn't want them to think less of themselves because they did. All I can say is that he has been consistent in his approach to the girls from the beginning, and it has nothing to do with winning or losing. And I like to think I have grown from his example. I also like to think that by using the word "magical" I'm talking about the way the season let me get to know him and how he helped me rescue my relationship with my daughter. Whatever people want to believe about the outcome of the game is fine.

In the end, I re-wrote the part about the championship. After eight tries, I had finally captured everything he wanted people to know about the championship game. Here is what I wrote:

The girls played like champions.
I believe God cheered for them.

After he read it, he smiled and said, "It's perfect. Thank you."

The Final Score

Two days after the championship game, our daughter brought home another envelope. Inside was an invitation to players and parents for the end-of-the-season banquet. Coach Miller wrapped up every season with a celebration, but this one also seemed to have the imprint of "God" on it. That's because of where it was being held: Marie's.

My wife, our daughter and I arrived at the restaurant on the following Monday evening, a time when Marie's is normally closed. My wife was able to be there for the banquet because her best friend's mom had improved from her stroke—at least enough so my wife's best friend could help with the evening classes. In fact, she returned just in time for my wife to also see the championship game. My wife cheered like crazy for our daughter and her team, and couldn't believe the change in me.

As we walked into Marie's, our daughter's teammates raced toward her, smiling. My wife was embraced immediately by the other moms while the dads welcomed me into a conversation with Coach Miller. Across the room, I saw him and Marie talking by the piano. I waved, and they waved back. A minute later, I watched my daughter and a few of her friends approach him and Marie. My daughter seemed to be asking them something, a question that led them both to smile and nod. I was ready to cross the room to join that group, but Coach Miller asked everybody at that moment to sit down so the celebration could start.

Marie's menu was traditional that night with servings of salad, garlic bread and a choice of lasagna or spaghetti and meatballs. Yet even in its seeming simplicity, the meal left everyone raving—a review that soared even higher after waiters and waitresses served Marie's homemade cheesecake for dessert. The dinner was a tough act to follow, but Coach Miller rose to the occasion as he shared his recap of the season. The best part was when he talked for at least two minutes about each of the girls, listing all the ways they contributed to the team as a player and a person.

Still, the girls stole the spotlight. When Coach Miller finished, the girls rose from the table where they sat together and headed as a group toward the front of the piano. They took turns thanking Coach Miller for all he had done for them. They thanked us parents for all of our support. They also made jokes about our "crazy cheering," drawing great laughs from everyone in the room when they recalled how the players on the bench first figured out that they were getting a standing ovation from the parent group *for* standing and cheering for their teammates on the court. Yet even as they joked about those moments, the joy in their faces showed how much they savored them.

They also thanked him. They thanked him for the notes he wrote them throughout the season—and how the notes made them closer as a team. They thanked him for the way he cheered for them early in the season, when he stood alone and cheered when they were losing, when he stood alone and cheered for things that no one else seemed to notice. They also thanked him for agreeing to a special request they had for this celebration. My daughter shared that request with everyone.

"Besides his unique cheering and his inspiring notes, and besides his love of popcorn and his fashion flair for white, high-top Chuck Taylor sneakers, the one thing that stands out about him is his voice," she said. "You hear his voice for the first time, and you think, 'Oh my God!' It's so-o-o amazing! Right?!"

Everyone in the room smiled and nodded.

"But have you ever heard him sing?" she asked. "Our team did one day when he was waiting for Coach in his office. We were passing by, and we heard this voice, and we thought it was someone on the radio. And it was him! We'd ask him all the time if he'd sing a few songs for us, but he kept putting us off, saying we had to practice, that *maybe* he'd sing for us after the season was over." She rolled her eyes when she said, "*maybe*." "So we asked him just a little while ago if he would sing tonight. And he said he would. So sit back and enjoy."

As he walked toward the piano where Marie sat, the girls all clapped for him. He shook his head and smiled at them, and they laughed and clapped louder. When they stopped, he surprised them with his own request.

"Before I sing, I'd like to ask a favor of the girls," he said. "There's some room for dancing up here, and I'm hoping the girls will get out here and dance." He paused and added, "With their dads."

The request stunned the girls momentarily. They looked at each other a little nervously, waiting to see what the others would do. Even as a dad, I realized that they were at an age when dancing with their fathers didn't rank in the top 100,000 things that crossed their minds to do. But children often have a way of surprising their parents. The surprise started when the girl who was usually the last one to get into a game walked toward her father and smiled. As the two of them moved to the dance floor, three more girls approached their dads. Then the room filled with girls heading toward the tables where their dads sat. When my daughter reached me, she laughed and said, "Did you put him up to this?"

"No," I said. "Not at all. But ever since I told him about taking dance lessons, he has always joked that he would pay anything to see me dance."

She laughed and extended her right hand with a flourish.

He had already started singing "Just in Time" when my daughter and I reached the dance floor. Everywhere I looked, fathers and daughters just smiled at each other. And it wasn't long before the moms ringed the edge of the dance floor, taking pictures of their husbands and daughters.

During one part of the song, my daughter and I ended up right in front of him. I could see him smiling as he watched my steps, and I was certain he would give me a hard time when he had the opportunity. Yet in that moment, he gave me a thumbs-up sign. A short while later in the dance, my daughter smiled at me and said, "This is fun." As my heart melted, she added, "He really does have a great voice. He reminds me of that smooth, gray-haired singer."

"Tony Bennett?" I asked as he hit all the right notes.

"Yeah, that's him," she said.

"You should tell him," I said. "He'd be thrilled."

I looked toward the piano where he was singing. I smiled and nodded. He winked back.

When he finished the song, everyone stood and cheered.

Over Time

A few years have passed since that magical season. My daughter now has a life that extends even farther beyond the world of her mother and me. It's the way it should be for parents and their grown children. I'm just happy that I'm still a part of her life. And I'm ever thankful that I was led to re-discover the great gift of being her father.

I'm also grateful for the beautiful, special and capable woman she is. At the same time, I savor those occasions when she comes home, when she calls just to talk, when she asks for my advice, and when she needs to know that the person who always has cheered for her still does. It's all part of the bond that started when I first held her as a baby.

In those times when she still needs my cheers, I naturally think of the person who showed me the best way to cheer, who led me back to my daughter. The reality is that I haven't seen him since that post-season celebration. At the end of that evening, he complimented me on my dancing, delivering the compliment with a straight face. Testing his sincerity, I said, "So do I dance as well as you sing?" He smiled and said, "Without a doubt." And we both laughed. Then he handed me an envelope and asked me not to read it until I was at home. A second later, someone interrupted us and said that I was needed for a photo of the players and their parents. When the photo session ended, I looked for him, but he had already left.

At home that night, I read his note. It was the shortest one he ever wrote to me. And the heart of the note was this sentiment: "There comes a time when the final scores and the win-loss records fade for most of us. At least they have for me in all my years of being involved in sports. Instead, I remember people and my relationships with them, and their relationships with others. When I think about this season, I will remember a number of special people. Most of all, I will remember the great ride you and I had together. I hate to see the season end, but now that it has in such a special way, there are other matters I have to take care of. The likelihood is that you won't see me for a long time. But I'll be rooting for you. Take care until we meet again, my friend."

That was the last time I heard directly from him. I have to admit that I miss the times we shared, and I sometimes wonder where he is and when our paths will cross again. Yet I've also learned that there are mysteries in life—and in each of us—that I have to accept and wait for them to unfold. At the same time, I still feel his presence in my life. I still think of him and smile when I hear a Tony Bennett song, when I enjoy popcorn in a gym or when I see someone wearing white, high-top Chuck Taylors. And I still see him in all the people who were part of the journey of that special season: the players, their parents, Coach Miller, Dan, Marie, my wife and our daughter.

I also see him in the children I now coach. I share his stories with them. I tell them his thoughts on when God cheers. And I try to teach them to believe in the one guiding principle of life that I've learned from sports, faith and him: It's not just that *anything is possible*; it's even more so that *amazing things are possible*. And it can all start with just one person.

"I've seen it happen," I tell them. "Let's be that person for each other."

About the Author

John Shaughnessy is also the author of *The Irish Way of Life* and *One More Gift to Give*, a Christmas story. A graduate of the University of Notre Dame, he grew up in the Philadelphia area and lives in Indianapolis. A longtime writer for *The Indianapolis Star*, he is currently the assistant editor of *The Criterion*, the newspaper for the Archdiocese of Indianapolis. He and his wife, Mary, have three children, John, Brian and Kathleen.